Multiple Staff Ministries

Books by Kenneth R. Mitchell
published by The Westminster Press

Multiple Staff Ministries

*Psychological and Theological Relationships
in the Multiple Staff Ministry*

Hospital Chaplain

With Herbert Anderson

*All Our Losses, All Our Griefs.
Resources for Pastoral Care*

MULTIPLE STAFF MINISTRIES

Kenneth R. Mitchell

The Westminster Press
Philadelphia

Book design by Gene Harris

First edition

Published by The Westminster Press®
Philadelphia, Pennsylvania

PRINTED IN THE UNITED STATES OF AMERICA

9 8 7 6 5 4 3 2 1

Library of Congress Cataloging-in-Publication Data

Mitchell, Kenneth R.
  Multiple staff ministries / Kenneth R. Mitchell. — 1st ed.
      p.   cm.
  Bibliography: p.
  Includes index.
  ISBN 0-664-25027-0 (pbk.)

  1. Group ministry. I. Title.
BV675.M49 1988
253—dc19   88-10049
                                                        CIP

Contents

Preface

In 1966 The Westminster Press published a book I had written, a study of the problems and possibilities of ministry in churches with more than one ordained pastor on the staff. Despite a painfully cumbersome title, about which I received some friendly ridicule over the years, the book was well received. It has been out of print for some time, but letters and telephone calls still come, asking where it may be found.

At first I tried to guess where I might direct such inquiries, but several things happened to make me less and less willing to offer that kind of help.

For some years, I have been conducting workshops for members of multiple staff ministries in several different denominations, both in the United States and in Canada. In addition, I took part in a cooperative venture of the United Church of Canada and the Anglican Church of Canada, producing a set of study materials on multiple staff issues, including a lecture on cassette tape.

Such experiences made me increasingly reluctant to try to help people find copies of the original book, because I was learning so much more about multiple staff churches from conducting those workshops and recording that tape. The situations I knew about, and the observations I made, were enriched more than a hundredfold.

A second reason for questioning the wisdom of continuing to use the original book is the number of important changes that have taken place in the patterns of ministry since the 1960s. My own denomination just began to ordain women in 1956, and there were few women serving in local churches at the time of the original research. That pattern has changed sharply. Women ministers were in training in the continuing education settings where I worked; women students became an ever larger proportion in the seminaries where I taught.

The increased number of clergy couples in which both wife and husband are ordained ministers has also had an impact on multiple ministry, as it has on patterns of ministry in general. Many people find themselves attracted by the idea of a couple serving together in ministry, but by and large the effect of this development has been less than a happy one. Many people concerned with placement and personnel in churches argue that it is "more trouble than it's worth." Whether that assessment is accurate or not, the phenomenon has an impact on churches with multiple staffs and bears further investigation.

In the third place, my original book began as a formal academic research project. Although there is nothing wrong with that in itself, researchers must often "control their variables" and "keep the problem within manageable limits." I was no exception. I limited the study to churches and staff problems in which there were two or more ordained clergy on the staff. That meant nonordained Christian educators, ministers of music, business personnel, and other people likely to be found on a church staff were not mentioned, nor were their particular problems or needs considered. In a continuing series of seminars at Princeton Theological Seminary, one of the most interesting changes has been increasing attendance by members of these nonordained groups, people who play significant parts in the life of a congregation. I began to listen to the difference these staff members made, and to try to hear what their particular needs were.

Fourth, there is the fascinating issue of shifting metaphors about ministry. When I was undertaking the research and writing for that first book, the dominant metaphor about ministry at the time was the "pastoral director," the term used by Niebuhr, Williams, and Gustafson in their book *The Purpose of the Church and Its Ministry*. Though sharply questioned by some critics at the time of the book's publication, the metaphor of the pastoral director held up as the primary metaphor about ministry for a long time. It was succeeded by the metaphor of the "enabler" in the late 1960s, but that term in turn has fallen into disuse, and it is uncertain what metaphor may yet take its place.

The terms "overseer" and "bishop" have recently been proposed to indicate the minister's function as one who oversees the many ministries of a parish. The difference between these metaphors and the metaphor of the pastoral director is, in my estimation, relatively small.

Finally, I had begun to develop a new set of tools for understanding the issues inherent in the multiple staff. My original book was the only book about multiple staff ministry that took both a psychological and a theological look at what was going on. (That doesn't say much; there were not many books about multiple ministries in the first place.)

My psychological approach was based partly in individual psychology and partly in social psychology. From social psychology I drew concepts about roles and patterns of organization and applied them to church life. Not available to me then were the concepts, tools, and techniques of family systems theory. Shortly after the book was published I began to learn the family systems approach, and I quickly began to see how applicable it was to the problems of multiple staffs.

I began to build those concepts into the material I presented at workshops. It was obvious, both to me and to participants in those events, that family systems theory made sense out of staff situations that were otherwise mystifying. In addition, the family therapy techniques that grow out of the theory were unusually helpful in changing difficult staff situations.

Theologically, methods more than content began to change. In the seminary where I first studied for ministry, theology was taught as an almost entirely deductive process, and I remained stuck with a deductive approach for a long time. More recently some mental doors have begun to open, making theology increasingly a two-way street for me. Like many other pastoral theologians, I talked about the two-way street for some time before I began to be able to practice it.

It now appears that a new book that takes notice both of new knowledge and of profound changes in the church is called for. Some of the approaches I took in the 1960s are still valid, while others ought, I think, to give way to more helpful approaches. In addition, a new book might be more accessible; my writing is clearer than it was twenty years ago. And I have the chance to get rid of that awful title.

Those ideas are not entirely my own. Workshop participants and students in seminary classrooms have encouraged me again and again to rewrite the book. Those who have read it and then have listened to the material I have more recently included in my lectures have insisted that some way be found to put the new material in the hands of church staffs and other interested people.

I am grateful to all those who have stimulated this revision. In particular, I am grateful to a large and still increasing number of participants in the multiple staff seminars at Princeton Theological Seminary, in several study centers of the United Church of Canada, and under the sponsorship of various judicatories of the United Methodist and United Presbyterian churches. Herbert Anderson has offered numerous helpful criticisms. Presbyterian Counseling Service in Seattle has been generous with the use of office equipment. Several students and colleagues have read portions of the manuscript. To all these friends I offer heartfelt thanks.

1

Multiple Ministries

Multiple ministries—in which groups of people work together as the pastors, administrators, and other ministers of a congregation or some other particular expression of the church—are an intriguing and sometimes heartbreaking puzzle. Ordained clergy often dream of having partners, colleagues with whom to share thoughts, feelings, and responsibilities. They dream of creating a working partnership that will be a microcosm of the church, a way of demonstrating to the congregation, by working and living together, what the church is about in the first place.

But when such an opportunity finally comes, the reality is often disappointing. Sometimes the partnership fits beautifully, but too often the hoped-for partner turns out to be unreliable or a loner or a bully. The congregation plays a game with the pastors that is painfully reminiscent of the psychological game all children play: "Split the Parents." I discover aspects of myself of which I am ashamed. Perhaps it is I who am unreliable or a loner or a bully. What a discouraging discovery!

Although there is intense interest on the part of many ministers in the problems and possibilities of multiple ministries, only a very few people have studied the issues thoroughly; it is still possible to count on one hand the books about it.

A little over two decades ago, when I wrote one of those

books, it was based on two kinds of research: intensive interviewing with ministers serving together on staffs of churches, and library research to provide some conceptual tools for understanding the events and processes I heard about from the ministers I interviewed. Its title was *Psychological and Theological Relationships in the Multiple Staff Ministry.*

After that first book was published, I continued investigating multiple staff ministries and have now collected much more data. Some aspects of multiple staffs have changed considerably, others not at all. Some of the tools I used for understanding multiple staffs still seem quite useful, while others have been superseded by more relevant new concepts.

UNCHANGING PROBLEMS, NEW OPENNESS

Many staff relationships are marked by friction despite good intentions and efforts to solve problems. But various experiments, often called "team" as opposed to "staff" by those who participate in them, have resulted in surprisingly high levels of satisfaction and effectiveness. These team experiments may at first startle the observer unused to them, because they define problems and solutions in unusual ways and make little use of the organizational structures with which we are familiar.

Why do so many ministries begun with good intentions fail? Why do some experiments succeed? The most probable answer is not that the successful experiments use nifty management techniques from Harvard Business School, but that they have achieved something called "second-order change." I will define and discuss that concept in chapter 2; for the moment, let us say that second-order change involves refusing to accept that the problem is what it seems to be. We do not try to solve a problem: not until we have first redefined the problem itself.

To move us one step closer to the kinds of things happening in multiple ministries today, here are true but disguised accounts of three events, all of which have taken place since 1983.

We Quit!

It was Saturday evening at eight o'clock. Andrew Grayson looked around his study one last time before he headed home. Everything seemed to be in order. Tomorrow he had to preach at three services, for today was Easter Eve. At least he wouldn't have to conduct the Sunrise Service at 5:55 A.M. Associate Pastor Don Trimble would do that. (It was typical of Don to do something cute such as setting an odd time for the service. It probably wouldn't really begin until six anyhow.) But the rest of the services would be his, and they'd be a bear. Fortunately, his other associate, Warren Grimes, would conduct the worship services. All Andrew really had to do was preach and pronounce the benediction. He found himself wishing that Grimes had a more impressive speaking voice. Well, you couldn't have everything.

At least the staff was in pretty good shape and in line these days. The new Christian Education Director, Maureen What's-her-name (Andrew never could remember it), seemed to be well liked by the teachers and parents, even though she seemed rather unfriendly and a little too self-possessed.

One last look around, and then home to Myra. As Andrew closed his desk drawer, there was a knock at the door. Without waiting for his answer, his three staff members trooped in with grim looks on their faces. Warren Grimes spoke first.

"Andrew, I'm afraid we have bad news for you."

Andrew Grayson looked from face to face. "Myra? Did something happen to Myra?"

"Oh, no, nothing like that. It has to do with church business."

"Well, I should think it could wait until later. We all have a lot to do tomorrow, and—"

"No," Warren interrupted. "That's just the point. We won't be here tomorrow—or any other time, for that matter. We came to tell you that we quit!"

"You what? You quit? You can't do that!"

"We can, and we have. All three of us have talked with the placement committee, and we have decided that we can't take any more of your bullying and your domineering. We've each tried many times to get you to understand, and you simply don't—or won't. So we decided that the only way to get you to pay attention was for all three of us to resign at the same time and leave the entire church to you. We quit. We won't be around tomorrow."

"You can't do that. You'll ruin everything here, to say nothing of your own careers."

"We thought of that, and we talked with the placement committee about it. They're willing to work with us to find places for all three of us. They say that they have been trying to talk to you about the way you treat staff for some years now, and we aren't the only staff members who have been unhappy working for you. We may have something of a problem, but the principal problem is yours.

"Good night, Andrew."

And the three of them walked out, leaving the pastor to absorb what he had just heard.

A Telephone Conversation

The scene is a staff meeting. It's a large staff: four ordained ministers, two educational specialists, a minister of music (not ordained), and a business manager. Several assignments were made at the previous staff meeting. The pastor, a quiet, casual man with a slight regional drawl that accents his friendly and accommodating style, has just called for reports on how the assignments have been handled. He turns first to a minister appointed to the staff by the bishop the previous spring.

"Well, Howard, how about your report?"

"I don't have one."

"Y'don't? How come?"

"I don't owe you a report. I'm not answerable to you. The bishop appointed me to this pastoral charge, and I'm only accountable to the bishop. I'm one of the pastors here, not your flunky. I answer to the bishop."

"I see. Thank you. Would you all kindly excuse me a moment?"

The pastor turns to the telephone and dials a number.

"Hello. This is Pastor Black. Is Bishop White in the office? . . . Thank you. . . . Good morning, Bishop. Arthur Black here. I'm sitting in a staff meeting, and Howard Brown—you remember him—has just been telling me that since you appointed him to this pastoral charge, he is answerable to you and not to me. I'm going to hand the telephone over to him now, and I wonder if you'd be so kind as to tell him where you are going to appoint him next."

Pastor Black hands the telephone to a flushed Pastor Brown, and what Brown hears results in his abrupt departure.

The Team at Purvis Harbor

On a cold, bright Tuesday morning in February, eleven people drift into the office of First Evangelical Church in Purvis Harbor, get coffee or tea from a small table in a corner, and take seats around the very large worktable in the middle of the room. These eleven people are the seven staff members (four of them ordained) who serve the four-congregation Purvis Harbor Evangelical Parish, together with one member of each of the four congregations.

What will these eleven people do for the next three

hours? They will share information about what's happening in each of the four congregations. They will dig into the scripture readings suggested in the lectionary for the coming Sunday. They will discuss possible sermon themes and outlines that might emerge from study of the scripture passages. They will get the beginnings of sermon outlines for all four sermons. They will select preachers for the four congregations. Then they'll disperse to the various places their work takes them.

Purvis Harbor is a community of about 40,000 people, a fishing town with farms and forests for a backyard. Until about nine years ago it had four separate congregations of the Evangelical Church: one rather large church downtown, a smaller church in the suburbs, a tiny farmers' church at the south edge of town (which never could afford its own pastor), and a chapel near the sawmill, attended by some of the timber workers and their families. None of the churches were as healthy as they would have liked to be. But more recently things have changed. The four congregations attained enough unity to cooperate in hiring staff, and now seven full-time people, including four ordained ministers, are employed by the four churches jointly. The system works far better than anyone had hoped.

The team—that's what they call themselves—meets every Tuesday morning for three hours to prepare worship services for all four churches for the following Sunday. Lay people meet with them; the whole group studies the lectionary passages, discusses the pastoral needs of each church, takes note of what's going on in the various communities they serve, and hammers out a common sermon outline together with some notes about the various differences there ought to be in the sermons. It's a team effort every step of the way.

The team has other meetings, but no chair—or, rather, no permanent chair. A different team member presides each month, and no one is referred to as head of staff or senior pastor. Everyone, ordained and unordained alike, has equal voice and authority in the worship planning as well as in the rest of the pastoral work.

Comments

These stories illustrate three kinds of approaches to ministry where two or more people work together in the same setting, approaches not only different from one another in practice but also coming from sharp differences in ways of thinking about such ministries. The first two represent a staff approach in which there is clearly a senior pastor or head of staff who is perceived by almost everyone, including himself, as being ultimately responsible for the operation. If one were to imagine an underlying structure symbolizing this arrangement, it would surely be a pyramid with one person at the top. Other members of the staff are accountable to the senior pastor. What one does not know is the degree of their commitment to, and sense of responsibility for, the full-time ordained ministry exercised in that congregation.

The second story also represents a clash of ideas about the nature of multiple ministry in a staff situation presided over by a firm but not authoritarian head of staff, well respected by his associates. He has an excellent working relationship with them on the whole, but his firmness as an administrator shows through when a newcomer attempts to rebel. Despite the fact that this particular incident involves conflict and sharp action, the staff of this church is highly effective and productive, and the church is regarded as a pleasant, desirable place to work. Participants, with a few exceptions such as Howard Brown, do not yearn for another kind of relationship.

The third story, at Purvis Harbor, represents an egalitarian approach to ministry, the kind of pattern its participants call "teaming," in which everyone shares equally in responsibility for ministry. There is no head of staff, and the team senses no need for one. One of the ministers has more experience than any of the others, and in certain situations the rest of the team turns to him for guidance; but it is not expected that he will be the leader in any but a temporary psychological sense.

Many participants in multiple ministries live at none of these extremes. For many of us, the "pure team" approach would produce considerable anxiety because of its apparent lack of structure and accountability. (Actually, everyone is accountable to everyone else.) Operating in this way involves an immense amount of meeting time, and there are those who think investing so much time in meeting with colleagues undercuts time necessary for "actual pastoral work."

On the other hand, few would want to work for an Andrew Grayson. The staff approach to multiple ministry does not necessarily imply an authoritarian stance on the part of the person at the top, but that is what happens in Grayson's parish. Multiple ministry in the staff model sometimes casts its participants as merely impersonal extensions of the senior pastor. But it is a mistake to consider that a necessary consequence of the model.

Note that Pastor Black is not authoritarian, even though he takes firm and authoritative action. It is in fact Howard Brown who in this story illustrates the approach typical of an authoritarian personality.[1] Arthur Black acts quickly to protect his own functioning, but that does not make him authoritarian. The participants in this story work in a context that grants great power to bishops; it rewards authoritarian stances and behaviors quite frequently. In this particular story we see a nonauthoritarian pastor and an authoritarian associate in a structure that usually rewards authoritarian behavior.

The stories are true, though the names are changed; they all took place in the mid-1980s. The story about Purvis Harbor is reminiscent of some team ministries I encountered in Canada in the 1970s. It suggests that experiments in teaming (which take some very creative forms in Canadian churches) are spreading.

The story about Andrew Grayson is one of three stories almost exactly alike, one of which took place around 1960, one in 1972, and one in 1984. Notice the angry, almost stunning, form the rebellion took. That same intense anger was present in all three mass resignations. Bullying styles and angry responses to them keep recurring. There are those who regard the bullyragging of an Andrew Grayson and the frustrated, angry responses of his staff as a built-in feature of all multiple ministries organized on a staff model.

CHANGES SINCE 1962

Twenty-five years ago, the single most frequently reported problem in ministries where two or more people were working together was the personality clash between "senior pastors" and "assistant pastors." Senior pastors complained, with relative frequency, that other members of the staff were irresponsible, lazy, unreliable, and unwilling to pay attention to the consequences of their behavior in congregational unrest and irritation. Staff members complained, with equal frequency, that senior pastors were domineering, uncollegial, narcissistic, vain, and manipulative.

Those complaints are still heard often enough. But senior pastors and the staff members accountable to them also report satisfaction and effectiveness quite often, and these reports are corroborated by congregation members who observe the staff at work.

My own denomination, the Presbyterian Church (U.S.A.), pays a certain kind of attention to relationships between staff members, as do other denominations. (So did the two Presbyterian denominations that united to form the present church.) As a result, some changes have been made—and more are currently contemplated—in the denomination's Constitution.

For example, the category of assistant pastor (a minister nominated by the senior pastor and hired by the church session) has been eliminated in favor of the associate pastor, a minister called by the congregation and installed, as is the senior pastor, but in some ways accountable to the senior pastor. The presumed intent of this change was to provide protection for staff members so they cannot be summarily hired and fired without congregational participation. But in many churches, a committee formed to nominate an associate pastor carries out its search without any consultation with the church's pastor and may present a nominee to the congregation without the senior pastor's knowing the nominee's name until the committee reports. Legally, it has the right to do so, but such a practice creates severe stress. It is enough of a problem that it deserves separate consideration, and I shall give it that consideration a little later.

More recently, there have been proposals to eliminate the senior pastor, on the grounds that it is an authoritarian rather than an egalitarian designation. (In the Presbyterian Church, at least, it is an informal title; the technical designation is "Pastor.") Such proposals almost invariably have at their root a wish to remove authority currently lodged in the church's pastor. We should expect that in the future someone will propose other changes to further reduce the authority of the pastor of the church. In general, this process illustrates the constant tension between egalitarianism and authority.

Unfortunately, alterations of this kind have almost no power to make the kinds of changes in relationships at which they are aimed. Promoting a more participatory style, providing more equity in jobs and relationships, and in general solving the problems we are discussing here are all tasks that have little or nothing to do with changes in formal documents such as books of order, constitutions, or job descriptions. If careful research and listening, listening, listening over the last twenty years has taught me one thing, it is that writing or rewriting or changing a job description has no power to improve relationships in multiple ministries.

Observable Changes

Constitutional changes have little effect on the workability of multiple ministries, and difficulties of various kinds persist; the important changes that have taken place over the last two decades have had quite different roots. Two of these changes have to do with what are often called *boundary* issues in church staffs.

Women on Staffs

Twenty-five years ago I was not able to interview one ordained woman staff member. A few women were being ordained to ministry in the early 1960s, but they were not yet very visible in the life of the church, and few were on the staffs of churches. A large number of unordained women were serving on church staffs; but officials—both individuals and bodies—could easily equivocate about whether they were actually staff members.

That picture has changed. By now, many churches have ordained women on their staffs. But that fact poses a problem for women, for prevailing patterns now seem to suggest that staff positions are where women "belong." Women serve in staff settings often simply because those are the places where they can find jobs. The number of women clergy in such positions is unusually high; churches may welcome women to their staffs but are less likely to call them as pastor. In addition, the jobs to which ordained women are called tend to be the same jobs that unordained women "Christian educators" with less theological training occupied a quarter century ago.

In any case, a consideration of multiple ministry must now take account of the presence of ordained women on staffs. In part, this will mean paying attention to the ways sexism still makes the position of ordained women in the churches difficult.[2] Another possible meaning is that the symbolisms of pastoral ministry are undergoing subtle shifts. In one multiple staff workshop, the group (comprising both men and women) agreed that men tend to see multiple ministries in terms of *power* issues, while women tend to see multiple ministries in terms of *relationship* issues. Men, someone in the group said, tend to think that what women want is power, but women see themselves as wanting relationships. That difference by itself would have a powerful impact on ministry. But it doesn't exist by itself; there are also issues of sexuality, styles of "mothering" and "fathering," and others.[3]

Nonordained Persons on Staffs

Boundaries of multiple staffs are also shifting in another way, so that churches now count nonordained persons as staff members far more often than they once did. I once found it natural to write only about ordained ministers serving together on church staffs. I could not do that now. I could not even *think* that way now.

This is a highly welcome development; it pays considerably more attention to reality. But, like all openings of doors and reworkings of boundaries, it stimulates a certain amount of anxiety. Just where *are* the boundaries? We accept unordained educators as staff members, and perhaps church musicians, but what about secretaries or custodians? Various staffs attending the Princeton seminars I give have included members of all four categories, and they by no means exhaust the list. Recently I heard a pastor argue persuasively for considering the director of the church's day-care center a staff member. Enough changes have taken place in multiple ministry that it is now difficult to argue a case for including only ordained persons as full-fledged members of a ministering team.

Couples on Staffs

An increasing proportion of ministers are couples, both of whom are ordained. In a few cases, the two are ordained into the ministries of different denominations, but the majority are couples in which both are ordained in the same denomination. Very often such couples offer themselves for service in the same church, as co-pastors, pastor and associate pastor, or two associate pastors.

The number of couples seeking jobs as pastor and associate pastor is small. Most such couples do not believe in relationships in which one spouse has more authority than the other, and, even though they must sometimes accept such relationships, they try to avoid them because of the potential danger to the marriage, the work as pastors, or both.

A larger number seek to serve churches in which the two will be on a par with each other in terms of the political structure of the church. But even when there is political parity, there is seldom if ever emotional parity or parity of competence. A seminary professor tells the story of a couple in her denomination, in which the husband was a highly skilled man, while the wife, though talented, was unable to cope with the emotional demands of joint work in the parish. Out of love, her husband covered for her. She appreciated that on the surface but resented it at a deeper level. Both the work and the marriage suffered.

My faculty friend's story called to mind a couple of my own acquaintance where the shoe was on the other foot; the wife was far more stable and competent than her husband. Our paths have not crossed in recent years, but reports from the area where they serve suggest that he is holding back what could otherwise be a fine career for his wife.

The interpersonal dynamics of marriage and the dynamics of working together in a team are such that few couples are able to achieve both a satisfying marriage and a satisfying working relationship. There are, to be sure, exceptions, but interviews and observations make it clear that they are rare.

Supporting or Undermining the Ability to Work Together

Some changes have had a decidedly negative impact on multiple ministry. Perhaps the chief of these is denying the present members of a staff or team significant input in the choice of new members. Whether the process of searching for and hiring new team members is carried out by a bishop, a judicatory, or a congregational committee, the present staff, including the senior pastor, is sometimes kept in the dark until a final selection has been made. Few practices are a greater threat to the staff's ability to work together.

My own ongoing investigations over the last two decades have demonstrated that the single factor that helps teams and staffs to work most creatively and smoothly together is a search process in which the present staff has the strongest possible voice in the selection of new people. Such a voice given to present staff members, coupled with a strong voice on the congregation's part (each of those voices has been denied at one point or another in the recent past) is an example of shared power. Shared power almost invariably creates chances for everyone in a congregation to "own" its mission and its ministry.

The practice of keeping the present staff out of the search process seems to have arisen as a reaction to certain pastors who made highly personal selections of an associate or other staff member without any congregational input. Under the general rubric that "the executive has a right to choose his own team," some pastors have chosen assistants or associates who have worked out poorly in one way or another. Strong reactions to such a personal process are certainly understandable. Some church folk are sure it is a corrupt practice, as well it may be. Still, it is very doubtful that a process built on the conviction that the choice of an associate pastor is none of the pastor's business will ever build useful and creative staff relationships.

Development of New Tools

Twenty-five years ago, the number of "glasses" through which one could look at the patterns in multiple ministry was limited. Psychologically, there were studies about the way individuals used and responded to authority, and there were writings from some social psychologists about the ways in which groups functioned; but there were few if any psychological frameworks that spoke clearly and directly to the issues of people working together. One colleague suggested that some light might be cast on the subject from industrial management studies, but these turned out to be of little use.

What had not happened then, but has happened in more recent years, is the development of a new understanding of human interactions in small groups (and to some lesser extent in large ones). These studies of groups as "systems" operating according to a certain set of rules and principles emerged from two distinct but overlapping sources.

Tavistock Studies

One source was the intensive studies of group process undertaken by women and men influenced by the work of the English writer, W. R. Bion.[4] These scholars and practitioners formed a network that included the Tavistock Clinic in England, the Rose Hill Institute in Canada, and the A. K. Rice Institute in the United States.

Participants in events sponsored by these groups have an opportunity to learn, from their own experiences, some very powerful lessons about group behavior: how and why groups succeed and fail at maintaining their identities and their boundaries; how the ways in which members take on roles can be great helps or grave hindrances to the performance of a group's task; how every member of a group is responsible for what goes on in the group's life; and many other matters.

Underlying all these particular lessons lies the general lesson that beneath the conscious, thoughtfully directed life of every group there is a "basic assumption life," a set of thought patterns and behaviors largely kept out of awareness, so that groups, no matter what they are supposedly doing, are also doing something else: for example, trying to make a leader feed them and be responsible for their well-being.

These Tavistock studies, as they have come to be called, also explore the relationships between groups. From their "institutional" events, and reflections on them, comes a powerfully increased capacity to understand how and why ethnic minorities are the targets of disdain and prejudice —and also a capacity to understand the relationships between the general membership of a society and its designated leadership group. The implications for congregations and church staffs are clear.

Systems and System Theory

A parallel source of light on multiple staff ministries is offered by the application of the new and rapidly developing understanding of human interactional systems. Some of the issues raised by students of systems—boundaries and roles, for example—are the same as those raised by the Tavistock researchers, but systems theory differs significantly from group theory.

It is difficult for group theorists, for example, to discuss what happens in the life of a group when it is not meeting. (Some group theorists argue that a group has no life when it is not meeting.) Systems theory, on the other hand, considers the life of a system as an ongoing process in which significant events may take place even when no two members of the system are in the same spot.

Some theorists have focused on the communication patterns in systems and on the power these patterns have in determining the system's life.[5] Others focus more closely on the structure of the family, seeking to make clear how the maintenance of the structure sometimes preserves the system at high cost in terms of the health and happiness of its members.[6] Still others wrestle with the tension between membership and affiliation on the one hand and differentiation and individuality on the other.[7] These differences sometimes make systems experts sound remarkably unlike one another, but in fact they are largely differences in focus and perspective. Of greater significance is a set of shared underlying convictions about a system as an organic being in its own right, the importance of boundaries, roles, rules, and rituals in its life, and the difficulty of changing an individual in a system without changing the system as a whole.

If we are to use the tools of systems theory to examine multiple ministries, the first requirement is to get a grasp of systems theory. We turn our attention to that topic in the next chapter.

A THEOLOGICAL COMMENT

Is there any reason to assume that ministry exercised by groups is inherently better or worse than a ministry exercised by a single human being? At certain times in human history God has chosen to work through an individual to whom charismatic gifts for spiritual leadership have been given. We often remember a great event or a great era by focusing our memories on such a great individual, from an ancient Moses to a contemporary Martin Luther King, Jr. Our current preoccupation with self theory and our emphasis on individualism may lead us to give particular importance to single figures who provide leadership.

That is a dangerous pattern. The great individuals on which we focus were, more often than not, symbolic individuals whose names are attached to work in (and on behalf of) a group of people. The preponderance of the scriptural evidence is that God's basic relationship is to a *people,* not to a *person.*

Recently I heard someone remark that the word "saint"

does not appear in the singular in the New Testament. I checked; it is not exactly true. There is one occurrence of the word "saint" in the New Testament, but it's part of the phrase "every saint," which implies more than one (Phil. 4:21). (There are sixty-one occurrences of the plural word "saints.") The New Testament speaks not of individual saints but of God's gathered people.

Government by a single individual is a form God's people have sometimes used, although kings were originally given only because of Israel's stubbornness. The individual healing miracles of Jesus were given in compassion for suffering individuals, but always as signs of the kingdom. The evidence is in fact very strong that God saves a people, God chooses a people, God works with a people.

Still, leadership is often temporarily lodged in a single person. Pastoral ministry exercised in a single congregation by a single ordained person is not in itself a mistake. It does on many occasions lead to the *High Noon* situation in which one person is chosen to serve as the surrogate for everybody's responsibility.[8] The difficulty with the *High Noon* pattern is that it invites the individuals who participate in it to view themselves as little messiahs. But it is also a workable pattern, with years of historical examples to attest to its value and worth.

The church and its institutions are so enamored of the pattern of individual leadership that theological education gives almost no attention to functioning in groups. Seminaries are geared almost exclusively to train soloists, almost never to train ensemble players.

I am convinced that God's chosen way of working is with a *people.* Ministry in multiple forms, through teams or staffs, is a reflection of the church and thus a reflection of God's preferred way of working with us.

2

Learning a New Way of Thinking

To understand the events and processes in any ministry where two or more people work together, we need tools that will give us a way to understand how groups function. Neither individual psychology nor social psychology goes far enough toward providing a solid understanding of the behavior of people in relatively close relationships.

SYSTEMS THEORY

Some years ago I began to immerse myself in the study of families. It was already obvious that although work groups, no matter how intimate, were not families, they displayed some remarkably family-like characteristics. I discovered that both intimate work groups and families were examples of a broader category: human interactional systems—or just "systems," for short. One could get a better idea of how families and other groups worked by studying the new approach called "systems theory."

An increasing appreciation for this new way of thinking made it more and more obvious that here was a key to understanding the phenomena in multiple staff ministry, one that opened a door onto a vista both broader and sharper than I had previously had. Here, then, are some of the most fundamental principles for understanding how families and close-knit work groups function.

That Awful Word "System"

Many things about systems theory are enjoyable to study and to use, but perhaps one thing about it that is *not* enjoyable is its name. If authors who write about systems theory begin to cringe every time they have to use the word "system," how must readers feel who have to keep reading it?

Besides, for many people the word "system" has unpleasant meanings, even if one does not run into it over and over. Somehow it seems like an inhuman or even antihuman word. It carries with it a sense of something blind, a juggernaut that mindlessly crushes everything in its way. We sometimes imagine that "the system" works against our best interests, that systems have no concern for the human lives they discommode or even maim. "You can't fight the system" is a common and bitter complaint. When we pay attention to the whole system, does not the individual get too little attention?

Under some circumstances such suspicions are correct; a system can indeed operate in an inhuman or even antihuman fashion. Yet all organized human groups—families, service clubs, church staffs, manufacturing companies, labor unions, even informal groups of friends—have lives of their own and rules by which they operate. In fact, the life and rules of a particular group—its strengths and weaknesses, its problems and possibilities—make it unique just as every human being is unique.

We live most effectively in small groups and families when we can see the world around us not as a collection of unrelated elements—some of which (the ones directly related to us) may have some impact on us—but rather as a number of elements related to us and to each other in a subtle, complicated way, so we can anticipate that something happening between two elements somewhere else (perhaps far away) in the family nonetheless has importance for us.

That is really what we do when we drive automobiles or fly airplanes, at least if we drive or fly safely. We become aware of the interrelatedness of everything around us, even when it doesn't *seem* to be directly relevant to our own vehicle at the moment. A drunken driver in another lane or around the corner may have immense importance for me even if the drunk's car and mine never collide.

A system is therefore not something alien; *any group of human beings in regular contact with each other is a system.* What this somewhat forbidding word really means is that human beings who work together, live together, or interact with one another over a period of time develop patterns in their relationships. They come to expect certain kinds of behavior from one another; they try to get their own needs met in their interactions; they attempt to carry out the purposes for which the group seems to exist (although they perceive those purposes through their own particular ways of looking); they develop patterns that are designed to preserve the group. Some such behaviors create conflict and stress in the group or its members.

Those are relatively familiar ideas, and they are the basic ideas that underlie theories about "human interactional systems." One reason the word "systems" is so heavily used is that it gathers a collection of ideas under one roof, so to speak. It refers not just to families or to work groups or to churches or to communities, but to all of these groups. What's more, it reminds us that however different these various kinds of groups may be, they do have some things in common. Then, too, the word "system" reminds us that there are forces and pressures at work inside the group, the kind of forces and pressures that psychologists call "dynamics." Something is always going on, and, despite the differences, those goings-on resemble each other in various kinds of groups.

But despite the fact that "system" is a valuable word, using it or reading it will eventually become oppressive. I have therefore made a conscious effort to use other words wherever I could: group, staff, family, church, community. In most cases, the reader will quickly see that where I have written "group" it would be just as easy to say "staff" or "church" or "system."

General Principles

People have been studying these patterns long enough to make some statements that are generally valid about all human systems. The most fundamental of all those statements is this: *Systems behave as though they were persons with lives of their own.*

In addition, there are several other principles that in one way or another are implied in that first statement.

1. Systems regularly act to preserve themselves and to resist change.
2. Systems maintain both external and internal boundaries.
3. Systems are always internally interconnected.
4. Systems assign specialized roles to their members.
5. Systems develop rules and rituals in order to bond members to one another and thus to maintain and preserve the group.

The last two principles—the ones about roles and about rules and rituals—will be discussed in the next chapter. In this chapter we will consider the principles that are most strongly connected with the *organismic* character of systems, their capacity to look and act remarkably as if they were single living organisms.

Systems as Persons

Systems behave as though they themselves were individual human beings. How can that be true? First, recall the old saying that the whole is greater than the sum of its parts. An individual human being is more than merely the sum of the cells that make up a human body. In the same way, a family is more than just a collection; it's a living being, and it has a life of its own that is more than merely the sum of the lives of the individuals that make it up. Everything else we have to say about systems is based on this fundamental idea.

That statement has some odd implications. For example, it implies a system may make decisions that are not necessarily the decisions any of the individuals in it would make. And this is often just what happens. We shall see other similarly surprising implications as we go along.

Self-Preservation. Like an individual human being, any group will under most circumstances act to preserve itself and to restore the balance of forces within it if that balance is disturbed. The theory says it this way: *Systems always resist change.*[1]

Someone wishing to intervene in an utterly evil society, such as one built on apartheid, to force it to change, would of course not be welcomed by the authorities. But suppose you and I wanted to help a church in trouble to improve its functioning. Maybe we were even invited to come in and help. The trouble is that systems make few if any distinctions between healing, helping, crippling, modifying, and destroying. Any kind of change, whatever its intent, is perceived by a system as threatening, and change will be resisted by the system even when many individuals within the system are in favor of it.

Look, for example, at a particular church staff. It consists of Pastor Jerry and Associate Pastors Barbara and Jim. There is a scheduled staff meeting every Wednesday morning at eight thirty involving these three pastors plus the director of music and the church secretary.

Barbara has for months voiced annoyance that Pastor Jerry is never on time for a staff meeting. Typically, he arrives fifteen minutes late, but often even later. The entire staff has speculated endlessly about the pastor's behavior, ascribing it to Jerry's poor ability to organize, to his need to show everybody how important he is, and to several other factors. Primarily, however, they are all angry because the pastor's behavior is so rude. Barbara has repeatedly and politely voiced her feelings (she has been "elected" to do so; in working groups, a woman is often unconsciously chosen by the group to express feelings), and the staff as a group has asked Jerry to be more considerate. Nothing has worked. Jerry continues to be late and to treat everyone else as though their time were far less valuable than his own.

After five months of this, Jim decides to try to change things. At the next staff meeting he waits for ten minutes, and when Jerry has still not arrived, Jim announces that he will not wait any longer. His policy, he says, will henceforth be to wait ten minutes for Jerry and then leave. He does not suggest that anyone else do the same, but simply that this is *his* policy. He leaves the building and makes some pastoral calls. The next day he finds out how his move paid off: Jerry mentions casually to him in the hall that staff meetings are now scheduled to start at nine instead of eight thirty.

Given the circumstances, the staff makes a prediction to each other. For two weeks, they speculate, Jerry will show up on time or even a little early for the nine o'clock meeting. After that, he will once again be fifteen minutes or more late. And so it happens.

As long as Jerry heard nothing but complaints, the system did not change. When Jim changed his own behavior, it caused a small change in the system. Notice that Jerry changed his own behavior as little as possible and merely decreed a change in starting time, which he soon violated.

When Jerry arrived for a nine o'clock staff meeting at nine twenty-five (on the third week of the new schedule), he found the meeting room empty. The staff had gone about their business.

It is not hard to notice that the system as a whole

attempted to change as little as possible throughout this whole course of events. At first, the system, through one of its members, complained. No change had actually occurred. Then a change was not just proposed but actually took place. The system acted to make sure that the change would have as little impact as possible. (People accepted Jerry's changing the time of the meeting and his refusal to change his own behavior.) The whole system did not change until everyone adopted the pattern Jim had suggested.

If someone who has a particular function essential to the life of a system disappears, the system will invariably attempt to maneuver another person in the system into carrying the function. That rule seems obvious and natural enough if we are thinking of visible and necessary jobs. The company that has lost a switchboard operator or a president will obviously try to find a new switchboard operator and will hire or promote a new president. Less obvious, but just as true, is the fact that some families need a "bad child" so much that when the current "bad child" in the family is sent off to reform school or prison by the authorities, the family will then "elect" another child to be "bad."

The purpose of such maneuvers is to restore balance when the system senses that balance has been disturbed. Any change in a system will be countered by some effort on the system's part to remain the same or as close to the same as it can. Systems theorists call this the "principle of homeostasis," from Greek roots meaning "to stay the same."

Some congregations seem to need a "financial objector," someone who will always argue against (or at least question) every increase in the budget. Suppose that someone who has been fulfilling that function in a particular congregation moves a thousand miles away and transfers membership to another church. What happens? Usually, someone who has previously supported budget increases becomes the objector. How the new objector was "nominated and elected," and how and why he or she "accepted the office," may remain a mystery. But that such things happen, and happen frequently, is undeniable.

But although some congregations need a "financial objector," others quite clearly do not. Some churches get along very well indeed with consistent budget growth and without a watchdog. In fact, if someone who has a tendency to question every proposed budget increase comes along, that person may be shut out in some subtle (or not-so-subtle) way.

Self-Consistency. One almost eerie feature of all this is that a church (or a business organization, or a family) will retain its character of needing or not needing a financial watchdog throughout a number of personnel changes. It is rather like the fact that a human being retains a certain appearance and personality despite a complete change of cells every seven years. So there may be several changes in pastors, and people may move into and out of a community or a church, and yet the need (or lack of need) for a particular type of person in the church's political structure will persist.

In 1955, a particular church was pointed out to me as a problem church in its denomination. In 1985, despite the fact of four pastoral changes in the intervening thirty years and a 97 percent turnover in membership, that same church was once again pointed out to me as a problem church. Fewer than 20 of its then 700 members had been members in 1955, and none of them had a particularly strong voice in the life of the congregation, yet this was still a problem church, and its problems were exactly the same ones it had had in 1955. This is not a rare occurrence; in fact, it is common.

When we bring our focus more specifically to the multiple ministry, we shall encounter situations in which it is expected that a change of staff—the dismissal of an associate or a clerical staff member, or even of the pastor—will solve the problems the church is experiencing. It won't; it seldom if ever does. But the fantasy that it will do so persists, and it is nearly impossible for those in charge to consider any other approach.

Boundaries and Associated Issues

Every human group has boundaries around and within it that divide the group both *from* the rest of the world and, internally, *into* its component parts. The boundaries are remarkably like boundaries in political geography. Political boundaries may be marked by some natural phenomenon such as a river or the crest of a mountain range, but sometimes they are entirely created by the work of politicians and surveyors, like the state line between Wyoming and Nebraska. So it is with the boundaries of human groups. We may not be able to see them, but they exist nonetheless. They are created by the people within them, to divide what is inside from what is outside and also to make separations between the individuals within them.

The people in a close-knit group, often without knowing that they are doing so, control the degree of ease with which its boundaries may be crossed. They may be very easy to cross or almost completely impenetrable. Sometimes the control of boundaries is a conscious act, as when churches admit people to membership. Sometimes the crossing of boundaries "just happens," as when the eleven-year-old is "followed home" by a stray dog that quickly becomes a beloved member of the family. In such cases, it is unlikely that the family is even aware that it has boundaries. It is not that the boundaries are not controlled when a pet is adopted, but that boundary issues are kept out of conscious awareness.

Internal boundaries—which involve permission within the system to move from one status to another or to control one's own physical or psychological space—are just as important as external ones. In a family, individuals may experience everything from complete lack of personal privacy to privacy so great as to be better described as isolation.

In churches, the control of external and internal boundaries may be in the hands of a particular group of people. Or it may be technically in the hands of one particular group, but actually in somebody else's hands. It's also observable that some churches make their boundaries quite tight and are known as "not very friendly" churches. Since the people already inside the boundaries may know one another quite well and enjoy very pleasant relationships, they may be deeply puzzled when from time to time they hear the "unfriendly" accusation.

Enmeshment/Disengagement. Some groups organize themselves so that the external boundaries are very difficult to cross, while the internal boundaries are permeable to the point of being almost nonexistent. Inside such a system a person characteristically has little privacy. There is considerable pressure to conform, almost always in behavior and often even in one's thinking. The tight external boundaries make it difficult to enter such a group and make it equally difficult to leave. Families and other groups that fit this description are called "*enmeshed* systems." Enmeshed systems also include such diverse groupings of people as nations, ethnic groups, and churches.

At the other end of the scale from enmeshed systems we find "*disengaged* systems," groups whose external boundaries are loose and easily permeable but whose internal boundaries are tight. It is easy to belong to a disengaged system and hold on to one's individuality. Privacy is highly valued, but strangers are often easily made welcome. Sometimes it's possible to see these differences in whole societies or cultures. In the Netherlands, homeowners almost never close the curtains on the windows to the living room, and everyone passing by on the street can see in. But the doors between rooms inside the house are always kept closed.

People who grow up in an enmeshed family may view the disengaged family as attractive because of its apparent freedom, and those who grow up in a disengaged family may view an enmeshed family as attractive because of its apparent warmth. The families we grow up in, which are the groups we know best, provide the foundation for the ways in which we participate in other close-knit groups encountered in adult life. Thus, growing up in an enmeshed family may make a disengaged church or church staff look like an attractive place to work, but at the same time we "know our way around" far better in an enmeshed staff, and we are likely to behave in ways appropriate to an enmeshed family.

Most systems exist somewhere along a line between pure enmeshment and pure disengagement. There are few pure types.

Gatekeeping. Even when boundaries are loose and permeable, they are still maintained. The maintenance of boundaries requires *gatekeeping,* a process controlling the crossing of boundaries into and out of the group. With any system—a family, a local congregation, a social group—it is often useful to develop an answer to the question, How does a person enter or leave?

Selecting a particular person or group of persons as "gatekeeper" is by no means unusual. Not all groups appoint particular persons as gatekeepers; in some cases, everyone shares the gatekeeping function equally. But the larger a group grows, and the more enmeshed it turns out to be, the more likely it is that a particular group of people are (consciously or unconsciously) assigned to be gatekeepers.

The gatekeeping function in larger or more complex groups may also be guided by a set of principles or rules, Those rules tend to be spelled out more clearly if the group has, as do most churches, a conscious political structure,

but left unarticulated if, like most families, it has none.
(Families do have a political structure, but it is seldom
conscious.)

Interconnectedness

The principle of interconnectedness may be easier to
grasp by means of a visual image than it is with words.

Some years ago a maker of playground equipment
began to offer for sale a new device. Made largely of ropes
tied together at various points, it looked like a small dome,
about four feet high and seven or eight feet across at the
base. At the points where ropes met there were small
"platforms"—pieces of wood an inch thick, four or five
inches wide, and about eight inches long. It looked like a
miniature geodesic dome.

Children played on this device by standing on one of the
little wooden platforms. If you bounced up and down on it
there was a pleasant sense of controlled give. But it was
not much fun to play on alone. The whole point was that
when other children stepped on other platforms, the pull of
each child's weight changed the balance of forces in the
whole device. Keeping one's balance as other children
stepped on and off became a challenging task.

That visual image depicts the principle of interconnectedness. Every action taken by every person in the group,
and every form of pressure applied at any one particular
point, will have an effect throughout the whole system. It is
simply not possible to affect only one person or office or
job; whatever you do has an impact, however small,
everywhere in the system.

In the biological system that is the human body, the
effects of this principle are often visible. Many people are
aware that puffy feet and ankles may well be a sign that the
heart is not functioning adequately, even though there is
no visible connection between the heart and the ankles.

Members of any group, or outsiders working with it,

should never be surprised to discover that an apparently small change at one point in the system has engendered a noticeable change somewhere else.

In one church, there existed a room I'll call the Lucille Davies Room. It contained four or five expensive pieces of furniture donated to the church by one Norman Davies, who had been three times married and three times widowed. Oddly, each of his wives was named Lucille. Each time a wife died, Mr. Davies donated an expensive piece of furniture to the church in her memory.

The Women's Association decided to put all those pieces of furniture in one room. They called it the Lucille Davies Room and declared that it was to be used for no purpose other than Women's Association functions. No one was even to enter it without permission of the Women's Association. There was a key to the room in the church office, but no one ever dared use it. (The church's governing board, by the way, had never taken any action of any kind about that room; the Women's Association's claim was never confirmed but never challenged.)

Assistant Pastor Bill Bartlett, charged with conducting the Membership Class, procured the key and took his class (sixteen thirteen-year-olds) to examine the room. Upset that the assistant pastor (to say nothing of a group of teenagers) had entered "their" space, the Women's Association angrily pressed for Bartlett's dismissal—and got it. The pastor attempted to take over the Membership Class, but not one of the children would come. Ten years later, not one of those sixteen thirteen-year-olds (now twenty-three-year-olds) would have anything to do with any church.

In this story we actually see two principles at work. The first is the principle we have been discussing: a small change somewhere in a church (or other group) may have results that no one foresaw. But a second principle lies behind that one: *it is never accurate to attribute any major change in a system to only one cause,* as if there were a straight-line connection between cause and effect. That's called "linear thinking," and in trying to understand what's going on in a church it is almost always a mistake.

It is tempting to suppose that Norman Davies's pious memorial gifts were the cause of the alienation of sixteen young people from the church. Alternatively, one might want to ascribe that alienation to an assistant pastor's boldness, to an association's self-centered and legally unsound exclusion of others from church space, to a governing board with weak knees, or to some other factor. But the direct ascription of the alienation to a particular cause—linear thinking—is never quite satisfactory. All the factors taken together, rather than any single one, conspired to bring about the result.

Triangles

In any human interactional system, the basic unit, or building block, is the triangle. The other principles we have dealt with so far are so generally known that it is not appropriate to consider them the creation of any one particular person. Now, however, with the introduction of the idea of triangles, the picture changes. The concept of triangles as the basic building block of systems is largely the creation of family therapist Murray Bowen.[2] We need to understand some fundamental ideas about triangles.

The first such idea is that *all two-person groups are inherently unstable and seek a third element.* Every group made up of only two persons can survive as a dyad for a while, but all such groups have a natural tendency to pull in a third element. This third element may be another person; it may be a physical object, an idea, a hobby, one's job, or any of a number of things. To qualify as a potential third element in a group requires only that the "candidate" be something or someone in which I can invest significant interest. Such elements provide stability by offering a place (or person) we can turn to when the two-person relationship becomes too intense, too troubling, or too threatening.

Second, *the bonds between the elements in a triangle shift fairly constantly.* When the three elements in the triangle are all human beings, two of them are usually bonded to each other while the third is left out in the cold. But this arrangement is temporary, at least in any healthy relationship. Consider a family triangle of mother, father, and child. If the system is a healthy one, there will be moments when mother and child are deeply involved with each other, while the father is odd man out. Later, however, Father may take the child fishing, while Mother stays home. Still later, it's the mother-father bond that's important, and the child is left out.

The participants tend to feel comfortable with such an arrangement temporarily, but soon the one left out may begin to feel a strong desire to reenter and will find a way to demand some attention. This move will split the two-person combination and force a shift. That pattern repeats itself over and over, so that the identity of the isolated one shifts constantly.

Rigid triangles are signs of an unhealthy group. They occur when one person is consistently or exclusively the one left out. Sometimes a rigid triangle develops when the bonds between two of the members are exceptionally strong, or when one person is noticeably different (a gender difference, for example). A rigid triangle is unstable, because the left-out person either chooses to leave entirely or precipitates a fight or some other difficult confrontation in order to get a sense of belonging. (It often feels better to be the focus of controversy or to be a scapegoat than to be completely ignored.)

When two people in a triangle are having difficulties in their relationship with each other, they usually do what Bowen calls "triangling"—that is, each person in the troubled duo demands the loyalty and support of the third person. Consultants—management consultants in industry or marriage counselors—are quite familiar with this phenomenon. Two people who are not getting along will each buttonhole the outsider and try to get an ally.

When a group consists of more than three people, it can usually be understood more clearly by identifying each of the possible triangles and examining it. While a couple whose marriage is in trouble tries to "triangle" the counselor, the counselor is well advised to look into the whole marital system to see what triangles exist inside the family.

In staff settings, triangling takes place constantly. There is nothing wrong with that; it's normal. The church secretary is the isolate in one triangle, while the two pastors have much in common. The associate pastor and the youth group may form a tight bond, leaving the senior pastor temporarily out in the cold. Shifts in these triangles take place regularly. But often enough a rigid triangle develops, and someone is permanently left out. I recall one church in which the organist and the church secretary, both charming, self-assured women in their fifties, formed a workable triangle with the elderly, widowed pastor. The pastor and the organist had an interest in music in common, the two women had many personal interests in common, and the pastor and the church secretary worked well together. Then the pastor slighted the church organist in some obscure way, and she formed an exclusive bond with the secretary. The pastor was for months the isolate. Nobody quite knew *what* was wrong, but everybody in the church knew *something* was wrong.

FIRST-ORDER AND SECOND-ORDER CHANGE

Making changes in the way a system operates is not easy. The usual way of trying to go about changing things is what I have called *first-order change.* Earlier, I promised to be more specific about the terms "first-order change" and "second-order change." The idea that there are two orders of change comes from systems theorist H. Ross Ashby. Essentially, first-order change refers to the minor changes that take place as a result of the ordinary and relatively constant information a system receives much of the time. Second-order change is the transformative, major change in a system in response to serious disruptions. For example, the on-off cycle of the heating system in a house as the air temperature warms and cools is a series of first-order changes. If a major cold snap occurs, the occupants of the house may reset the thermostat: second-order change.[3]

In a church or church staff, first-order change may take a number of forms. One well-known form is getting rid of somebody. If we fire the troublemaker, we suppose this termination will solve our problems. I recall a midwestern church that, in the course of eight years, had five assistant pastors. Each one seemed to have a serious enough flaw that replacing him with a shiny new model would make the necessary change. Some observers call this the Henry the Eighth approach, because the churches involved change staff members the way King Henry changed queens. Many former staff members in such churches attribute the whole problem to a selfish and jealous senior pastor, but that is often a mistake. Systems thinking reminds us that even a domineering senior pastor cannot get away with such behavior except with the collusion of other church authorities.

Another form of first-order change involves rewriting the formal rules: job descriptions, bylaws, books of order, constitutions, procedure manuals. If we prescribe how things are to be done, and write protections and requirements for fairness into the processes and procedures, we think we shall be able to make major changes. As I have already suggested, it doesn't work. Not that it does not induce some change; it simply does not induce the changes we are hoping for. The group will fairly quickly rearrange matters to undercut the intended change. Most of all, such changes provide a formal, legal refuge or court of appeal. The cost of using such machinery is always undesirably high; what we really want is for the system to change without our having to use such expensive, cumbersome, embarrassing strategies. Such efforts are often important, however, for we would not even have what we have without those formal documentary changes.

First-order change involves making amendments to the rules, but having somewhere in the background a fixed and invariable set of hidden rules about the ways in which it's legitimate to change the rules. One keeps on playing the same basic game.

Second-order change means playing a different game. In order to achieve second-order change, we have to change what systems theorists sometimes call the "meta-rules," the hidden rules about how the rules can be changed, the hidden rules about which changes are legitimate and which are not. When second-order change is made (or proposed), participants in a system often sense that things really are changing (and that it will be difficult if not impossible to undercut the effects of the change), and they may become uneasy or even angry. All they wanted to do was to "play the game better" or perhaps "get a referee with better eyesight," but now it feels as though they are not even playing the same game. It feels that way because it's true.

When a particular staff relationship is in trouble, it is almost invariably the case that first-order change will not do away with the trouble. Things may change briefly, but the same old difficulties will soon break out again. Second-order change is likely to do away with the trouble, but participants in the situation will resist it as strenuously as they can, even though they desperately want relief from the trouble.

Occasionally columnists such as Ann Landers or Abigail Van Buren publish letters in which the person seeking help sets out a painful and difficult problem but proceeds to forbid the helper to suggest this form of relief or that. "Don't tell me to get counseling (brush my teeth/cut off my ex-wife's credit cards/refuse to let unwanted visitors in the house) because I can't do that." Almost invariably the forbidden relief is some form of second-order change. Almost invariably the meaning is: I don't want change *that* much.

SUMMARY

This chapter starts us with an essential tool. Most people grow in their awareness of the power of this tool gradually. We tend not to realize how much new light understanding things—families, churches, communities —from this new perspective sheds until we come to grips with some of its implications.

One such implication is that in most conflict situations there are almost never any real villains. To be sure, there is evil abroad in our world; the concept of sin is not outdated. But a major conflict in a human system is almost never the result of someone's having made an utterly malicious or evil move. A failure of a program is seldom if ever the result of one person's mistaken decision or failure to act.

There is a saying that "all that is necessary for evil to triumph is that good men do nothing." (We should no doubt expand that saying to include both genders.) It fits in perfectly with the approach we have been discussing. We usually recognize its truth in general and resist its implications in particular. A lynching in the 1930s somewhere in Dixie was not to be laid solely at the feet of a few Klansmen but of the whole community, and perhaps of the whole nation. When a group of which I am a member does something I don't like, and I don't raise my voice, I'm responsible for the actions of that group.

The Old Testament records faithless behavior, particularly on the part of various kings in Israel and Judah. Although the kings came in for their share of blame from the prophets, it was not the kings personally but Israel or Judah who were usually called faithless. Israel as a people went into exile.

3

Roles, Rules, and Rituals

In the previous chapter I discussed some of the features of systems that make them resemble human beings. I mentioned homeostasis: the fact that systems display a very strong tendency to remain the same wherever and whenever they can. They maintain themselves, attempting to make sure that they not only survive but change as little as possible.

It's a toss-up whether the attempt to survive or the attempt to remain unchanged is primary. Ordinarily, the two go hand in hand; not changing is a means of survival. But that is not always the case. A group will sometimes pursue a particular course unchanged despite the presence of clear evidence that plowing straight ahead will pose a threat to survival. Historian Barbara Tuchman, in her book *The March of Folly,* cites the story of the Trojan horse as an early version of this phenomenon and then shows us how folly played itself out with the popes of the High Middle Ages, the British Parliament at the time of the American Revolution, and the U.S. Government vis-à-vis Vietnam.[1] Tuchman points out that in each situation, those in charge had ample evidence that the course they were following would have disastrous effects upon the country and upon themselves. They continued with their folly. The historian is somewhat surprised at this, but it's doubtful that someone with an understanding of systems would be so surprised.

Often, however, survival takes on primary importance, and at those times a group will (often very reluctantly) make changes in the way it functions. In any case, families and other groups always put an enormous amount of effort into the task of maintaining themselves.

How do they accomplish that task? Three major ways will be discussed in this chapter: (1) assigning people to perform specialized *roles;* (2) making and enforcing *rules* of behavior for participants; and (3) developing repeated patterns of behavior—*rituals*—to which emotional, intellectual, and sometimes spiritual meaning is attached.

What gives roles, rules, and rituals their power? The answer is at least threefold: *they regulate, provide a sense of identity, and bond members to each other.* Those functions, though distinguishable, overlap and reinforce each other.

The regulating function is the most obvious, particularly with regard to rules. (The Latin word *regula,* from which our English word "regulate" comes, means "a rule.") Behavior in any group, small or large, is almost invariably subject to rules of some sort. Roles and rituals, too, serve to keep order, to regulate a family or a church or a society. When people fill their roles adequately and do not step outside their role boundaries, the family knows what to expect from them and is getting, by and large, what it expects. Rituals, in part because they are by definition patterned behaviors, also regulate what goes on.

Roles, rules, and rituals also provide a sense of identity for the whole group. It is a particular family's roles, rules, and rituals that distinguish it from other families, that give it its uniqueness, and therefore permit its members to say "we" and to mean "ourselves and nobody else—*this* family." Roles, rules, and rituals are, for this reason, boundary-maintaining devices. They delineate the uniqueness of a group clearly, so that its boundaries are clear.

The third function, providing bonds between members, derives from the second. To the extent that members of a group can say "we" and know who and what they mean by that pronoun, they are provided with bonds to one another. At times such bonding works effectively even when there are tensions within an organization. Perhaps the most familiar example is that of the siblings who quarrel among themselves but put up a strong common defense when under attack from the outside. Speakers of a particular language may experience similar bonding, for every language is actually ritualized verbal behavior. When I know how I am expected to behave (what role I have), and how my behavior fits in with what I can expect of others, I also experience a sense of connection to those others who recognize and honor my role among them.

ROLES

In theory it's possible for everyone in a system to perform most if not all the tasks necessary for the group to survive. But it doesn't happen that way. *Most groups develop a need for specialized tasks and assign particular people to perform those tasks on a regular basis.* People take on roles. The role-assignment process takes place both out in the open and underground at the same time.

The assignment of roles requires a "political" process in which the group "nominates and elects" someone to take a particular role, and the nominated person "accepts" the office. (I use quotation marks because the process doesn't usually look like a normal political process, but I use political language because it best describes what's really going on.) The election may be out in the open or hidden from everyone's awareness. When it is hidden from awareness, participants deny that it is taking place. Someone in a difficult or unpopular role may want to insist that the rest of the family (the church, the group) "forced me into it. I didn't want to do it," such a person will often say. "*They* insisted." Group members, on the other hand, may sometimes have a stake in insisting that the person who has taken on a particular role has done so entirely of his or her own accord. The important fact is the one omitted by both: that in assigning/taking/accepting such a role there is collusion between the group and the nominee.

Herbert Anderson and I, in our study of loss and grief, pointed out that a family sometimes "chooses" one of its members to organize and manage the family's behavior at the time of a death in the family.[2] Such a person can also be said, in some senses, to have volunteered for the job. But later, that "grief manager" may complain bitterly of never having been given the opportunity to grieve.

The roles people take or are assigned operate at three levels: the formal, the informal, and the tacit. Choosing people to fill formal roles is always a process out in the open, choosing people to fill informal roles may be either out in the open or hidden, and choosing people to fill tacit roles is almost always a completely hidden process.

The three levels I refer to here are derived from my earlier work on contracts.[3] Any aspect of human relationships that includes the expectations we have about the behavior of other people operates on these three levels: formal, informal, and tacit. Contracts—agreements about what we shall do in relation to other people and what they will in turn do in relation to us—are expectational in character. So are roles. In fact, roles are essentially based on a kind of contract about the place individuals take in a particular social network or system.

Formal Roles

Formal roles are immediately recognizable in the whole culture and can usually be named in one word: queen, secretary, mother, sheriff. People enter such roles by election, appointment, or, in a few cases, inheritance. Whichever way it happens, the entry into the role almost invariably has something public about it. Ceremonies such as inaugurations, installations, and investitures often mark the taking on of a formal role. Not always, of course: the role of mother or father is entered into without such a ceremony.[4]

Formal roles often carry with them a clear understanding of responsibility and accountability. As a rule, they also carry with them some expectations so widespread and well-known that questioning them or even discussing them is usually unthinkable. Not in the sense of moral outrage, but unthinkable in the literal sense of the word: nobody in the system knows exactly how to think about it.

Roles such as pastor or associate pastor are of this kind. Most members of a church with a multiple ministry are, on the one hand, fairly sure what the pastor's responsibilities are and what those of an associate pastor are. They may even know where those responsibilities and accountabilities are spelled out in a formal document of some sort. But alongside these clear understandings there exist expectations (loaded with feelings) about pastors and associate pastors. One of the most familiar of these is the often-heard complaint of someone recovered from an illness that the church paid no attention during the illness. The *associate* pastor called frequently, but somehow that did not count.

Efforts to alter the way such a pattern works will often take the form of public announcements about the staff's responsibilities and areas of concern. Such efforts constitute what I have earlier called first-order change: redefining terms without essential change in the system. First-order change involves very small payoff for considerable work and is usually not worth the effort.

Informal Roles

Informal roles are the roles invented and used by the people in a particular system to make it function smoothly and are often identifiable as answers to questions. Who sells stamps in this office? Whose turn is it to take out the garbage? Who is preaching next Sunday?

Pastors may ask other staff members or members of the congregation to undertake such roles. "The Scout troop needs one more dad to go on an overnight next Saturday; can you help out?" "I've been doing the worship bulletin myself, but my time's getting filled up. Could you take over the preparation of the bulletin beginning next week?" Participants in the life of a church are free to accept or reject such role assignments. (But there may in fact be a rule lurking in the background that makes it extremely difficult to say no.)

Informal roles are not particularly tied to the structure of an organization; no organizational chart would show them, nor would a careful analysis of the structure of a particular system—a church, a business organization, a family— reveal them. They exist out of immediate convenience or necessity; in fact, one key aspect of informal roles is that they can be added, altered, or subtracted without any substantial change in the structure of the group.

Tacit Roles

Tacit roles are not talked about, not assigned openly, not accepted openly; yet clearly they exist. They function to meet important but unacknowledged needs. It's usually impossible for those supposedly in authority to assign such roles, and yet they are taken and used for the psychological health or the survival of the group and the individuals in it. The person who somehow maintains morale in an organization occupies a tacit role. So do the people who often function as hidden but definite gatekeepers in a church congregation. (If *they* haven't accepted you, you aren't accepted even if you've been a member for five years.) In a family or a staff, the person who pours oil on troubled waters, so that conflict does not break out openly, is occupying a tacit role.

That last illustration also allows us to notice this about

tacit roles: people who play such roles usually procure something—survival, comfort—for the group, but they may do so at a price that goes unrecognized. The pourer of oil on troubled waters guarantees that open conflict will not break out, or that it will be downplayed if it does break out, but the gain may be bought at the price of avoiding important issues (perhaps loaded with possibilities for conflict) that threaten the group. If they are never allowed to surface, we may pay a terrible price for ignoring them.

Does the person who plays a tacit role also do so at personal cost? That's always possible, but the price may be very hard to see. People in a tacit role very often undertake it in order to meet some psychological need; it is their half of the collusion. We tend to function in groups and families in such a way as to try to meet our own needs for comfort and emotional sustenance. That may cost us something in the long run, of course. But it is not necessarily the case. A colleague reminded me that a pastor we both knew took on the tacit role of cheerleader in his congregation. His efforts to keep enthusiasm at a high pitch may have cost him or his family something, but it is difficult to tell whether that is really so.

It is important for those who live and work in any kind of human system to identify the tacit roles which they themselves and others take on. The difficulty is that we usually have a huge stake in keeping tacit roles out of awareness, so that when someone identifies a tacit role, it is very likely that others will flatly deny it, or deny it more subtly by simply ignoring the new knowledge and acting as if it had never been offered.

Problems with Roles

"Families function best when there is flexibility about sociobiological roles, clarity about structural roles, and equality of emotional roles."[5] Although all three kinds of roles are visible in church staffs, it is the structural roles that occupy most of the participants' time and energy.

Clarity about structural roles in a church staff or any other work situation is a prerequisite for good functioning; one might think that was self-evident. In its simplest form, it calls for everyone involved to know "who does what."

But I have seen a surprising number of situations where such clarity is not only not present but seems to be deliberately avoided. A school with about fifteen faculty members and a clerical and administrative staff of more than twenty was "organized" on the principle of avoiding structural clarity:

> Newcomers were for long periods of time kept in the dark about where they could get the most basic kinds of help
>
> It was difficult if not impossible to trace the source of serious mistakes and get them corrected
>
> Power was concentrated in the hands of one clerical employee who was "elected" to have all the important information

As you might suppose, there were fairly numerous complaints about this state of affairs. Yet when the president of the school moved on to become the head of a charitable foundation, and a new president paid serious attention to the complaints, his quick and effective moves to rectify the situation (made after careful consultation with many people) were criticized as destructive of the school's traditional "human" values.

Now we need to add another principle—that *what actually happens is what the system intended to happen.* Of course, not everybody in the group intended for things to happen this way, but the group as a whole operated so that such things would be bound to happen. Since that was so, we have to ask what the advantage was to the school to have things arranged in this way.[6] In the same way, what is the advantage to the churches whose staffs are organized on a similar principle? (There are lots of these churches.)

RULES

Every system regulates and maintains itself by means of a set of rules, acknowledged and unacknowledged. The rules govern an amazingly wide variety of aspects of life within the group. There may be rules governing such matters as:

How information may be shared, what kind of information, by whom, and with whom

Who may be in relationship to whom, under what circumstances, and with what restrictions

What are considered honorable ways to earn money, appropriate foods to eat, and, in general, how individuals may legitimately sustain their lives

How persons of opposite sexes are to relate to each other in both sexual and nonsexual situations

How the physical space available is to be apportioned among the members, and to what purposes various spaces may be put

How the time available is to be apportioned, and what times may be devoted to various activities

What members are supposed to know, how they are supposed to learn it, and at what pace

How play is to be defined, which aspects of life may be treated playfully and which may not, and with whom playful relationships may be permitted

How the system will protect itself and its members from threats to psychological or physical survival and well-being

What tools may be used, what materials are appropriate for use by members, whether help of any kind may be accepted, from whom, and on what terms[7]

These categories were originally developed to refer to whole cultures, but there is ample evidence to suggest that smaller groups, such as congregations, church judicatories, staffs, or families all make rules covering the same general territory.

Acknowledged vs. Unacknowledged Rules

Some rules are completely out in the open, acknowledged by everyone; others are unacknowledged, underground, and may even be denied by members. Evidence of their existence is easily found, however; all one has to do is to look at the way the system actually operates.

The acknowledged rules may be a well-known aspect of the whole cultural milieu. This is the case for the statutes of a city or a state. Every group of people that is a part of a particular political unit is expected to obey the laws, and not knowing them does not excuse us from obeying them. There are other kinds of acknowledged rules, too. A staff or a family may design acknowledged but unwritten rules for itself in order to keep functioning smoothly.

Unacknowledged rules are kept out of awareness, but they are enforced. In a denomination that did not use the office or title of bishop, one minister received the unofficial but widely recognized title of "Bishop of the Red River." (I have changed the name of the locale.) It was clearly understood that no congregation in that area would call a pastor without securing the "Bishop's" approval. The minister in question denied that there was any such rule operating in that area, and so did many other clergy, yet it was absolutely clear to a very large number of observers that the rule was not only in operation but was rigorously enforced.

Similarly, it is often the case in local congregations that the pastor has veto power over the work of the congregation's nominating committee, but "it would not do" to acknowledge that rule.

What in one group is an obvious, out-in-the-open rule may be an unacknowledged rule in another. There are families in which rules about modesty are discussed and kept very much out in the open, and others in which such rules are hidden. A standard rule of thumb is that *observing* gives you more accurate data about the rules than *asking* what the rules are.

The rules of either kind control the behavior of members of a group in matters stretching from how one deals with strangers through how the space in the house is organized to the feelings one may legitimately express. Consider the following: "Client files may not be kept out of the locked file cabinets overnight." (A completely public rule, written down in a procedures book.) "Do not discuss our family's financial affairs with anyone outside the family except the banker." (A spoken rule, often reinforced by repetition.) "Every tub must stand on its own bottom." (This doesn't look exactly like a rule, but it has a clear meaning, and that meaning is a rule: "Never accept help from anyone.")

The Power of Rules

Rules have bonding power as well as governing power. The healthy use of rules to reinforce a group's bonds and to regulate its transactions is dependent upon the following factors:

The extent to which the rules *meet the needs,* not only of the group for orderliness and reliability but also of the individual members for emotional expression and gratification within that general sense of order

The *flexibility* of the rules, their ability to shift slightly to take differing circumstances into account

The *adaptability* of the rules, their ability to be applied to different persons in the group

The *visibility* of the rules, the group's ability to admit openly that there *are* rules and that *these* are what they are

The *unambiguous nature* of the rules, leading to the ability of members to know exactly what they are and how and when they will be applied

The *consistency* with which the rules are brought into play in similar situations

But not all rules are used in a healthy way. In some cases, the way rules are used may indeed provide a bonding force and keep transactions under control, but they will do so at a price. The rules with the greatest power are never spoken. There are always unspoken, unacknowledged rules; and these have immense power within a group precisely *because* they are unacknowledged. If everybody obeys a rule but nobody admits that it exists, the rule itself cannot easily be challenged. To state the rule openly is to bring its validity up for consideration, and that comes very close to pointing out the nakedness of the emperor.

Almost always, any aspect of a group's life kept hidden has the most power: unacknowledged rules, tacit roles. As to roles, the hierarchy of power is that the tacit roles are more powerful than informal ones, and informal ones are more powerful than formal ones. Similarly, unacknowledged rules are more powerful than acknowledged ones. The bylaws of a particular congregation are almost never the primary rules by which the system is governed.

Unacknowledged rules can be found in many schools and other institutions; they also serve to keep rule-making power in the hands of rule enforcers and to make their jobs easier.[8]

RITUALS

Rituals, which have tremendous bonding power, are used in a wide variety of situations. Each family usually celebrates Christmas with its own particular ritual, and the Christmas Eve service at a particular church often follows the same pattern year in, year out. Birthdays may evoke rituals in families, churches, or company offices.

Some rituals have a defensive purpose of some kind. They serve to help groups or families or individuals within them to negotiate situations that present some kind of difficulty. The difficulty may not be a critical one, but just a moment in life that carries some emotional stress. Thus, rituals are frequently used when a new person enters a family, when a significant person leaves, or when people are in the process of trying to create a new constellation of people, such as in marriage. They may be used at times of major personal changes, such as puberty or retirement. Some observers have suggested that even such happy occasions as birthdays, Thanksgiving celebrations, and Christmas festivities are marked by rituals because of the hidden but definite stress they involve.

Rituals may be carefully codified and prescribed in a formal way, and even described carefully in writing, as in the worship or prayer books published by various denominations. Strict adherence to them may be required in some churches, and they may be acknowledged as embodying or representing the basic meanings of the church's existence. Earlier, I spoke of rituals as having a strong part in providing a sense of identity; but in some cases the ritual *is* the group's identity. So it is, for example, with the Episcopal Church and its *Book of Common Prayer.* Elsewhere, rituals may be just as carefully described and defined, but the group may treat them with far greater laxity and may have a less urgent sense of connection between its rituals and the identity of the group, as with many Presbyterian groups.

When two comparable groups come in contact with each other, each is likely to find the other's rituals alien. At such moments we almost always disregard the fact that rituals are human creations and treat our own rituals as if they had a meaning validated by God with an approval denied to all other rituals. At the very least, we often focus on the rituals of others to prove to ourselves how odd these other people are.

To one of our jointly taught classes in the pastoral care of families, Herbert Anderson posed a question: "Is there anybody here in whose childhood family the Christmas presents were opened on Christmas Eve?" Several hands went up. "And how many of you," he persisted, "married someone in whose family Christmas presents were opened Christmas morning?" Not only raised hands but laughter and groans greeted this question. Almost as if he knew the answer, Anderson asked a final question: "Did that create a problem?" And of course it had. Two rituals had clashed. Anderson, whose own marriage had had to blend those two different rituals, knew exactly how to illustrate the point; and he and I have both used those questions repeatedly since.

Powerful emotionality may be vested in such issues, perhaps most painfully when the clash is between two groups who once had a common ritual but have now come to different forms. It is sometimes easier for Episcopalians holding "high church" views to feel kinship with Roman Catholics than with their own "low church" fellow believers.

Recall what happens when a new pastor wants to make changes in the ritual familiar to a particular congregation. Many pastors ruefully report that their congregations have been far more willing to forgive doubts about matters of doctrine than to condone proposals to put the offertory after the sermon. It is sometimes difficult for the minister to understand that the congregation is acting in a way that's normal for a group that feels its own identity and cohesiveness threatened.

One feature characteristic of the way groups treat their rituals is the assumption that, for the most part, rituals do not have to be taught to, or shared with, newcomers. Rituals are dealt with as though both their worth and their proper performance are self-evident.[9] In a certain Iowa city, there is a street intersection that strangers to the city find frightening and confusing. Residents negotiate it constantly with no difficulty at all. A new resident who complained was told that everybody in town knew how to approach that intersection and "people who aren't from here have no reason to go through it in the first place."

Few things can make someone feel more like an outsider than the sight of a group of people confidently and unself-consciously performing a ritual that to the newcomer is complex and confusing. The insiders seem to have absorbed the ritual with their mothers' milk. Moreover, they seem to have little inclination to help the newcomer master the intricacies. This behavior is not unfriendly, though it may seem so; actually, it seldom if ever occurs to a member of a group that others may not already know how to participate. Ritual has immense power to draw boundaries, and thereby to provide members with a strong sense of the group's identity.

SUMMARY

Two chapters of a book can only provide the beginnings of an understanding of new ways of thinking about human interaction. The new discipline called "systems thinking" is growing rapidly, and there is already a library of important volumes in the field. What I have tried to do in these last two chapters is to lay a foundation for a new way of looking at families, work groups, churches, and particularly multiple staffs.

In the next chapter I will offer a disciplined framework that can be used to study a church and its ministerial staff. The methods of investigation are based on the principles in these last two chapters; as we work our way through the investigation, other principles for understanding church staffs and other "systems" will also become evident.

4

Studying a Church or a Staff

People working in multiple staff situations often struggle to grasp the nature of the situation in which they are working. At multiple staff workshops, I use an exercise that produces clarity and enlightenment. I function as a kind of coach, and the workshop participants are the researchers. For the purposes of this book, this chapter is my coaching, and the reader is the researcher.

The exercise consists of a series of questions. Depending on circumstances, the researcher can ask these questions through interviews with key people, through personal observation, through widely distributed questionnaires, or through a combination of these methods. At the workshops, participants were asked simply to develop for themselves the best answers they could to the questions. When more than one participant from a particular staff attended a workshop, the individuals were asked to develop their own answers and then compare them in a group meeting.

A number of workshop participants have reported using this exercise as the central activity in a church officers' retreat. Reactions to the exercise used in this way have ranged from high good humor to chagrin. Sometimes underlying conflict has been brought to the surface. But, always, participants have emerged from the exercise with a better understanding of the setting in which they work, and usually they have gained tools or insights to make important changes.

The questions had their origin in a similar list of questions developed by the late Thomas W. Klink for use in a course called "Systems Studies," offered to students in the Pastoral Care and Counseling Training Program at the Menninger Foundation between 1965 and 1970. Klink drew some of his ideas from Ludwig von Bertalanffy's *General Systems Theory*,[1] but the originality and creativity of this method of study was his own. What Klink articulated, at a time before this theory was creatively applied to human interactions, has turned out time and again to be relevant and powerful. After Klink's death I began to teach the course, revising and extending the list. The present form and content are my own.

Each of the sixteen questions is actually a number of interrelated questions focusing on a particular theme. The themes are deliberately presented in an unusual, seemingly jumbled, order; Klink and I found over the years that disrupting the expected order of inquiries in fact stimulated clearer perceptions and answers less burdened by the answerer's inner feelings or prejudices.

The questions are organized in a three-part form. The first part, printed in boldface italics, is the master question, the one that defines the broad subject area. Next you will see a number of subquestions and, finally, a discussion of the meaning and background of the area under consideration.

THE EXERCISE

1. Naming

What is the name of the setting? Does it have any nicknames? Any pet names? Names that indicate a theological stance? Do members refer to it by a name different from the one used by the general public? Are there any names that indicate dislike or contempt? How did it get its name? Did it choose its own name or was it named by someone outside? Are there any myths about its naming? (This question should be reviewed when working with the question about history found later in this list.)

In some cases, this question will not produce much that is helpful. But very often the self-understanding of a particular group is wrapped up in its name and in the history of that name. Names are sometimes a powerful indicator of hidden underlying structures. They may indicate a church's attitude toward itself, the way it imagines it fits into the world around it, a desire to proclaim or to hide its identity and operations, the way it wants to limit its operations or to leave itself open to a variety of them. It was not at all difficult, for example, to know what the Smith-Corona Typewriter Company's business was, or what the Marchant Calculator Company made, but who knows what the SCM Corporation does? There is a subtle but definite shading of intent between the name of the First Evangelical Church and the Bible Faith Evangelical Church.

2. Subgroups and Supergroups

What subgroups can you discern within the group you are studying, and what supergroups can you find of which this one is a member? In what ways do any of the supergroups influence or control activities taking place in the church you are studying? To what extent do conflict and cooperation exist between the group you are studying and the supergroup in which it is embedded? Examine these same questions with regard to the group you are studying and the subgroups within it. (If you're studying a whole church, then the principal supergroup may be a conference, a diocese, a presbytery; if you are specifically studying a staff, the principal supergroup will be the church's congregation.)

No particular group ever stands alone. Every group is part of a larger one, and most groups have smaller ones within them. Knowing this is true and being able to identify these larger and smaller groups will keep the researcher aware of the complexities involved.

3. Involvement

What is the nature of your involvement with this group? Do you have an official relationship? Do you see that relationship the same way members see it? What is the purpose of your study? Do others know you are making this study? If so, do they understand your purpose the same way you understand it? If not, why do they not know? If you are an insider, what do you know about the way in which outsiders perceive the group or vice versa? How can you expect your particular relationship to skew your conclusions, and how can you protect the integrity of your study?

The ideas and opinions of insiders are usually at least slightly self-deceptive. To be an outsider is to be able to see some things more clearly. (But insiders will say you are an outsider so you don't *really* understand.) Thus, working on the basis of observations is, for the outsider, somewhat more reliable than interviewing insiders. For the insider the interview method may be a bit more reliable, because in that case information from others tends to counteract one's own blind spots.

If you as investigator have an official position, it is necessary to acknowledge that. Holding an official position tends almost inevitably to skew the results of any investigation. You are likely to introduce, however unconsciously, some form of self-interest into your work.

The question is about *your* role in the system, and being

very clear about your relationship to the system you are studying is essential.

4. Space

How does this group use space? Are there "holy" spaces? Spaces where everyone regularly passes? Spaces designed to allow the entire group to come together? Spaces reserved for one person or a small group of persons? Spaces under the tight control of a particular individual or subgroup? (Do some places "belong" to particular groups?)

What is the overall psychological effect of the space and its use? Crowded or spacious? Simple or complex? Welcoming or forbidding? Does the entire space or some parts of it have a specifically "masculine" or "feminine" feel? Is most space multipurpose or devoted to one particular purpose? Are there formal and informal places? Relaxing places? Private places?

With regard to places allotted to employees and staff, are these adequate for the work staff members are expected to do? Are staff's rooms or offices easily accessible? Do they reflect the personality of their occupants, or is uniformity imposed?

Church groups (and other kinds of groups) usually make rules, overt or covert, about the use of space. The way in which space in a church is assigned, the way it is decorated, its accessibility—all give powerful evidence of the ways in which people who work there are expected to relate to one another and to the task.

5. Membership Boundaries

Describe the membership boundaries—that is, how does anyone know who is in, who out? Are those boundaries clear and well defined, so that it is easy to tell who is a member and who is not? Are the boundaries easy or difficult to cross? What are the normal modes of entry and exit? Are there modes of entry and exit not easily visible but tacitly acknowledged? Are there tests for entry? Under what circumstances do people usually leave?

Who are the gatekeepers at the boundaries? Are there both formal and tacitly acknowledged gatekeepers? Are there also gatekeepers who manage boundaries between one status and another? Is the control of the boundaries partially or entirely in the hands of outsiders? For example, do members of some larger organization have a hand in choosing who may enter *this* organization?

With respect to internal boundaries, how much privacy do members enjoy? How is privacy achieved? What is the balance between community and privacy? Are internal divisions of office and status clear and carefully maintained or casual and not easily visible? Can one move from one status to another? How is this accomplished?

Membership boundaries are only one kind of boundary. When we discuss time and space issues, we also get into boundary matters. The way in which any group manages and protects *all* of its boundaries is important to the life of the group. Membership boundaries, the way they may legitimately be crossed, the way people sometimes "illegitimately" cross them, who maintains them—all these are important indicators about the life of a system. Note that the rules, overt or covert, about how one crosses into an organization may be different from the rules about how one gets out.

Sometimes two kinds of boundary issues may overlap, as when a group meeting in a particular space is constantly interrupted by intruders. Such a group is having trouble with more than one boundary issue.

6. History

What is the history of this group? Can you see times of little or no change? Times of gradual change? Times of sudden change? Are some events in the history seen by members as times of a grand blossoming or a terrible wounding? Are myths attached to such times?

Is there a "birth myth"? Are there individuals or other groups that somehow seem like the parents of this one? Are there other major figures in its history?

How has the group, during its history, interacted with the historical changes in one or more of the groups in which it is embedded—such as the community or the denomination as a whole? Is there a history of conflict with other churches or their staffs? Has the church or staff essentially behaved as though it were not existing within another system? (For churches, this may mean operating as though the surrounding neighborhood had never changed, or operating as though it were a completely independent congregation despite being part of a denomination with an episcopal or presbyterian polity.)

Is there a history of inner conflict, or has the group been relatively conflict-free for most of its existence?

What or who are the symbolic ideas, symbolic physical realities (such as a building or a piece of important furniture), or symbolic persons that play a major part in the history? Can you discern what values or meanings they stand for? What symbolic patterns of repeated action (rituals) can you see operating? Do members talk about rituals once used but no longer engaged in?

Systems maintain themselves and express their values by means of a history, which usually intermingles factual accuracy and mythology. Mythology is a form of historical narrative in which an interpretation is given to facts (sometimes at the sacrifice of absolute factual accuracy) in order to express a particular value or a deeply held, deeply felt truth about the group. Such mythic interpretations are most likely to be found in the stories of a church's origins or in connection with the stories of major changes in its personnel or outlook, but they may be found inextricably intertwined with any aspect of history.

7. The Group as One Person

Can you imagine this group as one living human being?
Do not imagine a real person who is a member unless that
one person so powerfully symbolizes the group that you
cannot avoid it. Is the person old? Middle-aged? Young? A
baby? Once vigorous, now less so or even decrepit? Male?
Female?

Imagine a characteristic expression on the person's
face. Imagine the person in a characteristic body position
. . . in a characteristic activity. What do the facial expression, the pose, and the activity signify to you? What
impression would you be trying to give, or what truth
would you be trying to tell, if you used these metaphors to
describe the group to someone unacquainted with it?

8. Time

How does this group handle time? Can you discern
weekly, monthly, and annual cycles in its life? Are there
periods of low and high activity? Which of the periods of
high activity are scheduled to be so, and which seem to
happen in an unscheduled though regular manner?

Are there times specifically set aside for work? For
fostering interaction among members? Holy times? Times
for learning? Times for goofing off? What do the times
indicate about the value the group places on these activities? Do differences in role also mean differences in
expectations about how the person's time is to be divided?

Do starting and ending activities on time seem to be
valued? Are starting and stopping times especially precise
or especially casual?

Every group develops a characteristic way of handling
the limited commodity we call time. The relationship between time management, time consciousness, and the life
of a particular group is so intricate and complex that a full
discussion here is not possible. Yet grasping this particular

idea is very important. *The Silent Language,* to which I have referred elsewhere, is an excellent source.[2]

9. Rules

Can you list no more than ten and no fewer than five rules that you believe are generally known and acknowledged throughout the group? Now make a list of no more than ten and no fewer than five rules that you are relatively sure operate but the existence of which is generally not acknowledged or discussed by a significant number (not necessarily all) of the members.

Compare the two sets of rules. Allow yourself to speculate about what the comparison may have to tell you.

10. Future Image

Earlier, you were asked to imagine the group you are studying as if it were a single person. How will that person appear five years hence? Has the person remained unchanged? Aged more rapidly than might have been expected? With what stresses has the person had to cope?

11. Losses and Secrets

Can you discern any losses the group has undergone at any place in its history, either recent or distant? Are these losses openly discussed, or was it necessary to listen very sensitively in order to realize that they had taken place? As far as you can tell, how has the group (and how have its members as individuals) responded to the losses? Are the losses viewed as natural and to be expected or intrusive and unfair? What is the attitude with which the group responds? Does it seem to feel challenged? Defeated? Temporarily stymied? Victimized?

Similarly, have you sensed that the group may be carrying around secrets of some kind? Is there a portion of history kept hidden? Are there people in the history who somehow seem carefully neglected? Are there processes or persons in the present that do not get talked about? Do informants occasionally seem to be guiding you away from certain topics, or at least reluctant to discuss them?

Losses and secrets have particular meanings for a group, and sometimes the group treats significant losses as secrets. On occasion, unresolved feelings about losses (which may even have taken place before the birth of any present members) still have powerful influence over current operations.

In churches in particular, one event that may lead to such losses and secrets is the sudden departure of a member of the pastoral staff or ministering team. If you are an outsider, it may require special skill and sensitivity to be allowed to hear the story—or stories; there is often more than one—behind the departure of a minister.

12. Roles

What roles are important in the operation of this group? (Because this question and the next are related to material covered in detail in earlier chapters, I do not go into the same amount of detail in explaining them.) Make a list of formal, informal, and tacit roles that are used. For a thorough discussion of the concept of roles and of the three levels at which they function, look back at chapter 3.

It may be of particular value to add some notes here about roles you would have expected to find and did not find. Why do you suppose some roles are missing? Why did you expect to find them?

There are few questions as good as this one for giving the researcher a grasp of how a system actually functions, because the roles a group assigns to its members (no matter on what level) tell you what activities are considered truly important. If a staff needs a "troublemaker" and has elected a couple of people to that office, but doesn't seem to care about whether it has a "peacemaker" or not, you know something about the energy level and the anxiety level.

13. Triangles

What triangles can you see in operation? (This question is largely based on material in chapter 2.) Who is usually allied with whom? What persons seem to function in frequent isolation? Are there members who are particularly persistent in attempting to ally themselves with leaders so as to protect their own power and influence?

Every family or work group has within it a set of triangles: alliances between two people that perceptibly shut out a third person, at least temporarily. A healthy situation can be described as one in which the makeup of such triangles is constantly shifting, so that no two people are perpetually allied and no one person is perpetually excluded.

Triangles form in a number of ways. Two people sometimes become bored or threatened by their association with each other, yet must be in relatively regular contact. In this case, one of the two people in the pair may seek a temporary alliance with an outside person, leaving the regular, usual partner temporarily isolated. Alternatively, someone who is currently not closely related to or allied with anyone may come to feel that more power or influence over events can be had by breaking into an alliance that already exists and taking the place of one of its members.

14. Careers

What are the normative careers for members? Is there a "power career," whereby ordinary members move into roles or positions of greater power? What proportion of the members will be likely to move onto this career track? What proportion of the members will be likely to have a career in the group involving no status change at all?

How long might a person expect to be a member before his or her career would involve a role change? Are newcomers given jobs fairly soon? Are gender differences noticeable; that is, do men and women regularly have differing careers?

Are there careers *in* the group that can be expected to take some members *out* of the group, perhaps to active work or membership in a supergroup of some sort?

15. Values

Review the material you have prepared in your study thus far. What values do you believe this system consciously or unconsciously cherishes? List them. In each case, indicate how the group uses its resources and its energy to maintain these values and to express them.

The values important to a group may be expressed by stories, mottoes, jokes, and other seemingly unconnected material. The true values are of course to be seen in the group's behavior, particularly when coping with stress or conflict.

16. Vulnerability

Reviewing everything you have learned by undertaking the study thus far, can you identify the points of vulnerability? No group is completely invulnerable, and the way in which a given group organizes itself usually makes it vulnerable at some points more than others.

It is often helpful, in working with this question, to think back to the once popular television program *Mission Impossible*. "Your mission, should you choose to accept it, is to disable the operations of this staff within forty-eight hours." How would you do that?

Assuming that your overall intent is *not* to sabotage the group, what could you or others do to protect the vulnerable places?

In the several years of working with this valuable question, I have found that its value increases if the student temporarily assumes a genuinely hostile position and exercises as much imagination as possible. Step away from this question for a few days after setting up your 'attack." Then return to the question as determined to defend the group as you previously were to attack and destroy or disable it, using the same imagination.

When you have finished this *Mission Impossible* exercise, return to the question about values that you answered earlier. Does your work on vulnerability provide you with new insights into the staff's values?

SUMMARY

The information that comes from this exercise can be used in a number of ways. Perhaps, however, the doing of the exercise is such an end in itself that one is *using* the exercise while one is doing it. It is rare for a group to participate in this exercise (if they are studying themselves) without becoming sharply aware of things about the situation that need changing.

Tedious? Certainly, a full application of this outline constitutes a research project, and some aspects of research are always tedious. As with all such information gathering, you may sift through a lot of information before you begin to get a clear and valuable picture of your setting as a system. Putting what you have found in the form of a report may also be a long and involved project.

But there are useful and pleasant ways to conduct this study. The *Mission Impossible* question has several times made a church officers' retreat a lively, provocative time. A youth group, particularly thirteen- and fourteen-year-olds, makes an excellent research team on the way an organization uses its space, possibly because they come at the facts with fresh eyes, having far fewer presuppositions about how things are "supposed to be." Any one of these questions can be used by itself as a promoter of change.

Granted, these discoveries alone cannot entirely change

a group, but to the extent that they do so, the exercise may make change possible. In addition, when a group participates in focusing on the system to which they belong, they are put in a position where it is hard to avoid certain subjects that usually are not talked about. Thus, doing this exercise is a secret-exposing device; but it does that job relatively gently.

5

The Self-Study
of Pilgrim Church

In this chapter you will see a sample of the way one church studied itself by using the method described in chapter 4.

The staff of Pilgrim Congregational Church in Springfield decided to undertake a study of itself and the congregation it served.[1] The staff members gathered data and impressions separately and then pooled their results. In doing so, they asked two people—the church secretary and a seminary intern then serving as a member of the staff —to write separate reports incorporating everything that everyone had found or surmised. Those two then combined their reports to make sure nothing was omitted or distorted. That whole report is too long for this chapter; what I present here is just some of the material appearing under each of the headings suggested in chapter 4.

Under the heading "Comment" in some sections I offer my own reflections on the material prepared by the staff.

1. Naming

In addition to its formal name, Pilgrim Congregational Church is also known as Old Stone Church to many people in the community. One of seven churches of its denomination in this midwestern city of 200,000 inhabitants, Pilgrim is the only one that did not prominently display the name of its denomination, when that denomination was formed by merger in the late 1950s. Members of the church said they clung to the name because of its historic tie to the Pilgrims who settled in New England in the early seventeenth century. "It is a name rich in Congregational history," said one informant, "and we treasure the historical associations. Actually, we participate fully in the work of the denomination, and you'll notice that underneath our church name on the bulletin board outside we do put the denomination's name, although in smaller letters."

There are no other names by which the church is known. No one—absolutely no one—ever uses the abbreviation P.C.C. The only short form of the church's name is Pilgrim.

Serving this church is a staff made up of two ordained ministers, a seminary intern, a church secretary, a business manager (part-time), a custodian, and the minister of music (part-time).

Comment. This material has been slightly "translated." Since the actual denomination is not Congregational (or United Church of Christ) and the name of the church is not actually Pilgrim, I have had to make minor alterations. However, the renaming of the denomination, the church's reluctance to use the new name, and the historic associations all accurately reflect themes in the original study.

The report speculated at length on the meaning of the name Old Stone Church, concluding that it was probably meaningless. I doubt that; it seems likely that for some people, at least, the nickname suggested considerable conservatism—that the church was more conservative than it in fact was.

2. Subgroups and Supergroups

The staff at Pilgrim is of course a subgroup within the congregation as a whole, and two sets of people (see the section on space) clearly represent subgroups within the staff, probably the most important subgroups. Other subgroups visible within the staff include the ministers (which at Pilgrim includes the seminary intern) and all the other staff except the ministers. The minister of music refers to this nonordained group as the "Yeomen," but it appears to be her term alone. She, the secretary, and the seminary intern are the women on the staff. They do not appear to form a subgroup.

The ministers meet at eight thirty on Tuesday morning, and the rest of the staff joins them at ten. At this time the associate pastor conducts a brief service of scripture reading and prayer. After the meeting, the entire staff eats lunch together. The group culture clearly demands that all staff members stay for lunch. They bring food in brown bags; coffee is prepared by the custodian.

In the congregation as a whole there are three kinds of subgroups: official groups such as committees and the Church Council; several interest groups, some of which have formal names like the Gaffers (a weekly gathering of retired men); and groups more difficult to identify that seem to have a base in personal associations outside the community. These include a group seemingly made up of community activists who are not currently represented very much in the Church Council but have considerable power in the community at large.

The church is active in the affairs of the next higher judicatory (conference), and two previous conference executives have been elected to that post from the pastorate of Pilgrim.

3. Involvement

This report is being prepared by the whole staff. All of us have some stake in the outcome. The congregation is aware that this project is under way, because at least one of us has interviewed each member.

Our original purpose was to try to help ourselves deal

with certain tensions that have surfaced between two identifiable "gangs" in the staff. (See the section on space.) The experience of the two transcribers is that various members of the staff have asked us what we are including and how we are working together. We believe that other staff members would like to have more control over the final form of the report than our operating method permits.

We acknowledge that self-interest of various kinds may skew the results of this study.

Comment. I would guess that the transcribers are right in this last comment, and that these moves indicate some secrets in the life of the church. At this stage, one can't say for certain what those secrets are, but the person ready to think of the staff as a system will from this point on be alert to the presence of some kind of secret.

4. Space

The principal entrance to the church (except on Sunday mornings) is a double door from a side street. From this door one goes up eight steps to the main hall, or down eighteen steps to the lower hall. The most heavily used entrance to the sanctuary is at the end of the main hall. The Girl Scouts know this; that's where they park themselves at cookie sale time.

The staff occupies space in two distinct parts of the church building. The pastor, the church secretary, and the business manager are in a suite of offices reached by climbing the flight of stairs from the entrance, while the other staff quarters are reached by going down the much longer flight of stairs from the same entrance. No one shares office space. Within the staff, there is some apparently friendly banter referring to the "Upstairs Gang" and the "Downstairs Gang."

The friendly character of the banter may be more apparent than real. It is clear that there is considerable resentment on the part of the Downstairs Gang, with the exception of the custodian, over the more luxurious quarters occupied by the Upstairs Gang.

On the main level one enters the church secretary's office at the top of the stairs coming up from the street entrance. One can go through the secretary's office and out the other side to the business manager's office, and through that office to the pastor's study. The pastor's study also opens out onto the church parlor, which occupies almost the entire east side of the hall. Across the hall from the church parlor are a chapel and two education rooms.

On the lower level, the minister of music has an office at the bottom of the stairs. Essentially, this is a music library. Choir rehearsals are held two flights up, in a choir room off the upper hall. The associate pastor has a small office at the far end of the lower hall, and the intern's office is under the staircase at that end.

The business manager's office is a kind of "holy space." No one would look askance at you if they found you in the pastor's study; they would assume you were waiting for the pastor. But people found standing around the business manager's office receive suspicious looks. Office equipment, both there and in the secretary's office, is strictly off limits to anyone except their "owners." Not even the pastor dares to use the copy machine in the secretary's office. The door between the secretary's office and the main hall is kept locked when the secretary is not in it. The custodian, the associate pastor, and the pastor have keys to that door.

Underneath the sanctuary is a large multipurpose room. It serves as a dining room, a gym, a meeting room for the Boy Scouts, and a polling place at election time.

Noteworthy in all this is the comparative location of the offices of the associate pastor and intern, on the one hand, and the offices of the pastor, secretary, and business manager on the other. The doors to the associate pastor's office and that of the intern are not visible from the lower hall. There are people in the church who have only the vaguest idea of where these two offices are.

The "feel" of most of the offices is noteworthy. The pastor's office is warm and private and lends itself to conversation. The associate pastor's office is cramped and not connected to the central heating system; an electric space heater is used to keep the room warm. The intern's office is somewhat larger, but its ceiling slants from a height of eight feet at one side to a height of four feet on the outer wall. The custodian has made a very warm and comfortable place for himself in the furnace room, furnished with two old easy chairs and a small refrigerator.

Staff meetings are always held in the church parlor around a large table. The Women's Association has complained about this use of the parlor and has several times asked that staff meetings be held in the pastor's study; but he has resisted this request. He gives two reasons: (1) he believes it important that the Women's Association not develop any further proprietary feelings about the parlor, and (2) he believes that staff meetings should be held on "neutral turf."

Rooms in the building, including the parlor, have an informal atmosphere, with the exception of the chapel and the sanctuary. The chapel is more formal than the sanctuary; it has dark coloring and a richly colored stained-glass window. The sanctuary is rather plain and light-colored, with yellow translucent windows but no stained glass.

Comment. The original report was very extensive, including a floor plan of the church building. The fact that this question elicited such a long and detailed response suggests that use of space is a problem-laden area in the system.

When the remarks about the location of offices were presented to the whole staff, the pastor vigorously denied them and insisted on running a check with several church members. He came to a subsequent meeting rather sheepishly admitting that the location of these offices was indeed almost unknown to members of the congregation. The comments on the relative placement and size of staff offices illustrate the value of this approach.

To balance things somewhat, it is interesting to note that the pastor displays sensitivity to some space issues by insisting on holding staff meetings in the parlor. While the parlor may not be the best place for a meeting, the reasons the pastor gives for using it are sound.

5. Membership Boundaries

Membership in the staff as well as in the church as a whole is clearly defined. The pastor has made very clear to anyone interested that he considers the staff to comprise the seven persons listed earlier, and that staff meetings involve all these people on a regular basis, although not every staff member is present for the whole meeting.

It is easy to become a member of this church, requiring no personal appearances before any board or committee, but only a conference with the pastor. Becoming a member of the staff is of course a more formal process. The selection of the present associate pastor was marked by considerable dissension, not because the associate pastor was disliked but because several people believed the pastor was being bypassed or shortchanged to serve the interests of an ultraliberal faction in the church. The pastor has expended considerable energy to dispel this notion and points out that he works well with his associate.

Although the church works hard to give the impression of being warm, friendly, and open—and succeeds, for the most part—there is an inner core of members who maintain some control, particularly by virtue of being well represented on the nominating committee. There are three couples in particular who seem to be tacit gatekeepers, and those who have not been accepted by these couples tend to feel on the edge of things even when they have numerous other friends in the congregation.

At Council meetings, motions are frequently made to "cleanse the rolls"; that is, to remove from the list of active members people who have moved away, college graduates who have settled in some other city, and the like. Such motions are routinely made at each meeting and routinely defeated. (Since the clerk is a stickler for parliamentary order, the defeated motions do not appear in the Council minutes.)

Comment. It seems somewhat easier to cross into the congregation than to cross out of it. That may merely suggest warmth and friendliness, but it is likely to be tied to a sense that there is a downward membership trend and to a desire to stave that trend off or even deny it.

Staff boundaries are clear, and the sense of an executive group being present and in charge is quite strong. That's always a healthy element in a system even when some rebelliousness is also present. It must be remembered, of course, that the staff itself is responsible for the study.

6. History

The church exists because of a mission effort on the part of First Congregational Church not quite one hundred years ago. Some older members seem aware of this mission history, but most church members are indifferent to it. Pilgrim and First are the two largest churches of this denomination in town (about eight hundred members each) while the others all have between one hundred and two hundred members. There seems to be a sense of competition between the two larger churches. Research did not uncover any particular birth myth for the church.

The Golden Age in the church's life is largely thought of as having peaked about two years ago. Things are viewed as not quite so good now. This feeling is largely connected with the character of the surrounding community, which is changing fairly rapidly. For many years there has been a black community whose boundary is about six blocks east of the church's location. Pilgrim has several black members who live in that community, which is apparently very stable. The largely white community nearer to the church is changing rapidly, however.

One symbol of this shift is found in the Boy Scout troop that meets in the church. The troop has had a rule that all fathers of boys in the troop are members of the Troop Committee. Five years ago that posed no problem. Now, however, more than half the boys are in single-parent families and have no father living with them.

It seems difficult for the members of Pilgrim to talk about what's happening. People are frequently heard to say that "the community is just not as nice as it used to be." It is fairly clear that the change is a socioeconomic one. People of comfortable means are moving to newly developing areas on the northwest side of the city, and their houses are being bought by far less affluent newcomers, many of whom have moved to the city from a nearby rural area usually considered less cultured and less well off economically. What people appear to want to say is that the community is being invaded by white trash, but that's not a very nice thing to say, so people in the church tend not to say it.

The church's history up to this point has been one of steady, continued growth. No particular events seem to serve as markers of historical significance. Some people do regard as important the year that the church's budget and membership became big enough to justify calling an associate pastor. That was about ten years ago. Now questions are being raised about how long the church's situation will justify an associate.

The church takes pride in the fact that it has taken a seminary student as an intern every year for fifteen years. The "teaching church" designation thus earned was used by the search committees that located the last two pastors, and it is clear that a pastor not interested in serving as a supervisor for an intern would not be called.

There is very little conversation beginning "We always used to . . ." There are, however, rituals in the life of the church that seem to be losing their appeal, although the church is loath to give them up. One such ritual is a tableau of the Upper Room regularly mounted on Maundy Thursday for the last twenty-two years, managed by a retired professor of drama. He is now in his early eighties, and his health is not so good. People regard the inevitable day when he will no longer put on the tableau with a mixture of relief and dread. Once a drawing card that brought people from other churches, the tableau is now routine. To many, however, it symbolizes the church's long-standing interest in the arts, music, and drama.

The staff has little or no history. The pastor dates the staff as beginning last July, when the present intern arrived, and says, "Every time someone comes or goes, there is a new staff." The custodian says that the staff always seems the same to him, "like the ax that the lumberjack had for twenty-five years, which had seven new handles and four new heads but was still the same ax."

Comment. The foregoing material is a brief extract from a long historical study. What is clearest from the historical material is that this is a church thinking of itself as slightly over the hill, about to enter a long downward path. It has a few rituals that tie it to its history, but there seem to be few myths that have much power.

7. The Group as One Person

Perhaps because of the historical material that was worked on just before this question was approached, the image of the church as a person appeared as a vigorous middle-aged man looking prosperous and well-dressed, but with a cast on his foot, a cane in his hand (temporary?), and new and very thick bifocals.

He looks slightly disgruntled as he scans the horizon before him and seems hesitant to take the next step.

The staff, on the other hand, is imagined as a somewhat more vigorous man in his twenties, walking with the middle-aged man and impatient to get him to move more rapidly. One imagines this younger man encouraging his older companion to get a move on, saying, "You can trust me to guide you, and if you do trust me, we can move ahead faster." But the older man is as dubious as the younger one is impatient.

8. Time

The staff operates according to several time cycles. The weekly cycle includes, of course, the worship service on Sunday mornings, but it also includes the weekly staff meeting, which seems important to all. Other weekly cycles are encountered, but only two seem to have great importance: the choir rehearsal on Wednesday nights and the Boy Scout troop meeting on Tuesdays.

There are also daily time cycles. The two ministers are present throughout the morning but are hard to find in the afternoons, since they maintain an active calling program throughout the congregation. The afternoon is an intense time, however, since the church is across the street from a junior high school and makes its facilities available to junior-high-school-age children every afternoon from three to five. The intern and the custodian are deeply involved with these activities, and the intern serves as an informal counselor to many teenagers. (A minority of church council members regularly object to this use of the building, but the council has thus far reaffirmed the program by an overwhelming majority and seems to have the overall support of the congregation as a whole. The staff is very strongly supportive of these activities.)

One special time is the Wednesday evening volleyball tournament. Beginning on Wednesday evenings at "nine," three volleyball games are played. The games actually begin when choir rehearsal ends. Two thirds of the players are choir members, and the choir director is an avid participant. Other church members also show up. This set of games is never announced in bulletins or openly discussed in the church, but it regularly draws a group of eighteen to thirty people every Wednesday from September through June. No staff member ever goes to the volleyball games, and two staff members dismissed the games as an unimportant (because unofficial?) activity. Yet there are at least ten individuals whose primary contact with the church outside of Sunday worship is this tournament.

The "time culture" of the church demands that all activities begin on time. It is commonly accepted that no matter how important anyone is, scheduled activities will begin on time without that person. Twice the pastor stopped to chat with a parishioner in the hall on Sunday morning, and the associate pastor began the worship service without him. The pastor was neither surprised nor annoyed.

Comment. This area of investigation is rich; it is simply impossible to put down everything about the "time culture" of Pilgrim Church. The small amount included here is enough, however, to permit grasping in a preliminary way how the study of the ways an organization uses time may reveal something of the underlying nature of the organization itself.

9. Rules

Acknowledged Rules

1. Everyone is expected to be in the office by 8:30 A.M.
2. With regard to the services of the church secretary, the preacher for the coming Sunday has first call; after

those needs are met, things operate on a first come, first served basis.

3. Church groups and events are divided into three approximately equal sections, and each of the three ministers is responsible for attending all the events and groups assigned to him or her.

4. The church parlor belongs to the whole congregation and not to any one group.

5. There are no assigned places in the 24-space church parking lot.

6. The pastor preaches 36 Sundays each year; the associate pastor preaches 12 Sundays; the intern preaches 4 Sundays.

Unacknowledged Rules

1. The pastor's demands on the church secretary always come first, no matter what else is going on.

2. The parking space nearest the church door is reserved for the pastor.

3. The associate pastor is expected to know which meetings and events the pastor cannot attend, without being told, and to cover for the pastor without being asked.

4. The custodian has veto power over the use of any room at any time.

5. Although the church parlor does indeed belong to the whole church, the kitchenette attached to it is strictly the property of the Women's Association. Staff members do not use it. If they are preparing lunch for themselves, they use the larger but far more distant main kitchen.

6. The custodian makes out his own schedule; rooms and halls are cleaned when he decides they need it.

Comment. Only rules pertaining to staff operations and staff responsibilities are used in these lists; a similar list was constructed for the congregation. This time, however, it may be useful to focus on the staff and their relationships as revealed by this list.

When the list was presented to the whole staff as part of the report, the pastor denied that his demands on the church secretary came first or that a parking place was reserved for him. He complained that these items made him look or sound like a self-centered tyrant. The associate pastor, after insisting that the report was accurate, asked what made the pastor think that he was responsible for making and enforcing the rules. Startled, the pastor began at that moment to realize that there were rules created not by him but by the system. (Of course, he had accepted the benefits.)

Comparing the lists reveals that more authority is in fact vested in the pastor than he has asked for or consciously expected. They also reveal that power issues are important in this staff and, indeed, throughout the church. Everyone agreed that the judgment about the kitchenette was accurate and that the whole staff resented it. When asked why they had never challenged this apparent rule, they all professed to fear the anger of the Women's Association.

Staff members speculated whether there was any rumbling in the church about the custodian's power, but all decided there was not. Six months later, however, the Women's Association demanded that the custodian be dismissed because he would not follow the schedule for cleaning rooms and halls they had proposed. The custodian stayed, but the vote was close.

10. Future Image

Five years in the future, the person representing the congregation will have changed little. He will still be vigorous, but a little less so, and although he is not carrying a cane, he has considerable trouble seeing through his even thicker bifocals.

The staff appears once again as an impatient guide or

companion, but this time the staff is much older and seems quite tired.

Comment. This image seems to indicate that the church will "use up" the staff—wear them down, tire them out—but largely out of inertia rather than real needs the staff must meet.

11. Losses and Secrets

One major item stands out in this category.

The present pastor of the church is the seventh pastor to serve this congregation. The sixth pastor, who accepted a call to a church in Connecticut, is lovingly remembered. But the fifth pastor of the church is never discussed. If one asks about him, answers become vague: "Well, it's kind of hard to know what happened to Sam" (not his real name). Denominational record books show Sam is the pastor of a thriving church in Iowa, to which he apparently went directly upon leaving Pilgrim, where he had been for eight years. In terms of the way the denomination's polity works, the departure of the fifth and sixth pastors looks exactly alike: they received calls to other churches, accepted them, and went. That's also how other clergy near Pilgrim remember it.

But somehow the departure of this particular pastor is marked with painful feelings. One widow in her seventies, asked in an interview about Sam's departure, became tearful and said that she had expected Sam to bury her. A middle-aged couple looked angry and said, "He let us down."

At first it appeared that the fifth pastor had done something to offend people and had had to leave. But comments such as those of the widow just quoted led gradually to the conclusion that what people couldn't forgive was the fact that he had left them. The conclusion grew ever stronger: the congregation had never properly grieved Sam's departure.

It may be important to record that none of the present staff is acquainted with Sam or has ever met him, nor did we make any effort to contact him for this study.

Comment. This one incident makes clear how this approach can help create a useful picture. There was mild depression everywhere in the congregation, not particularly shared by the lively if conflicted staff. Was it possible that the ungrieved departure of Pastor Sam was an underlying factor in the mild depression? It certainly seemed so. Further inquiry made it clear that Sam had left at just about the time the surrounding community had begun to change. How do you grieve for someone who abandons you in a time of need?

12. Roles

The formal roles in the staff are the same as the job titles given earlier, and the informal roles are not particularly worth paying attention to. The tacit or psychological roles that exist in the staff are of interest.

There is a large share of "father figure" vested in the pastor. He is viewed as the ultimate source of authority, the one who must make decisions or countersign them if they are made by others. Moreover, he is seen as a kind of dispenser of goodies, the granter of privileges, the spokesperson of the staff.

Everyone was apparently comfortable with this role until the present seminary intern arrived. The intern is a secure, highly competent woman in her forties, married to a minister and the mother of two teenage children. She has been employed as an office manager in the local office of a major national brokerage firm and has been an active laywoman in the church. Two years ago she responded to the urging of her husband and several friends and entered seminary. In this internship she is more than three hundred miles from seminary and home.

In this setting she has the role of questioner, although the pastor would no doubt say "troublemaker." She has called into question almost every pattern that church and staff would have thought of as traditional. She has challenged the "father figure" image of the pastor and has asked openly where, if anywhere, the mother figure can be found. The pastor believes, but never says to her, that she is nominating herself as the mother figure.

The location of her office is unacceptable to her. She says she recognizes that she cannot expect to have the same office as the pastor but makes it clear that she cannot tolerate having her office hidden away on the lower level "not quite in the furnace room." She points out that the custodian's quarters, actually in the furnace room, are considerably more comfortable and spacious than her own.

Though polite and cheerful, she is assertive and vocal, seeming to take pleasure in the discomfort that the pastor and the rest of the Upstairs Gang feel in her presence. Her first sermon took the congregation to task for its "hidden sexist attitudes." She points out that the role of troublemaker is uncomfortable for her, but that she has a sense of self-worth coming from years as a successful business-woman which is now—she believes—under attack by this traditional, conservative congregation.

The staff and congregation are both experiencing discomfort. The role of questioner or challenger or troublemaker has never seemed needed in this congregation, and the church as a whole has little idea how to deal with people who choose such a role. Sentiments are heard that she should be "put in her place," but as the associate pastor said, "If she were twenty-three and just feeling her oats, putting her in her place would seem pretty easy. But this is a strong, mature, competent, attractive woman, with a happy marriage, two very attractive children, and a husband who supports her right down to the wire. She already knows her place and is comfortable in it. You're not going to *put* her anywhere." By and large, the feeling both in staff and congregation is that everyone will simply have to ride out the storm.

Comment. Apparently the church secretary wrote these paragraphs but she had to share them with the intern before they were presented to the whole staff. It would have been interesting to hear the conversation between the two of them when they first met to review this material.

If the staff wrestled thoroughly with even this single role question, it would open up a door for powerful sharing and perhaps even restructuring. As it was, the staff was moved by what they read to try to lead the congregation into some revised thinking about the role of questioners and trouble-makers in the life of the church.

13. Triangles

So many triangles exist that we cannot describe or even list them all. We point out a few that seem to us to be particularly significant.

The pastor–associate pastor–intern triangle is, we think, strong and healthy. We see the two ordained pas-tors of the church as a pair, with the intern left out. We see the intern and the pastor as a pair based on their supervi-sory relationship, with the associate pastor temporarily isolated. We see the intern and the associate pastor, as members of the Downstairs Gang, arrayed against the pastor. No one gets stuck in the isolated position for very long.

A not-so-healthy triangle consists of the pastor, the associate pastor, and the church secretary. In this triangle, the associate pastor is the perpetual isolate; he never seems to be able to claim the genuine attention of the secretary, who is always aligned with the pastor.

We also think we see a kind of triangle consisting of pastor-staff-congregation. Perhaps this triangle is not really made up quite this way, but what we perceive is that particular members of the congregation try to align themselves either with the pastor against a particular staff member or with a staff member against the pastor.

Comment. The staff was perceptive in their selection of triangles. As one might guess, the church secretary was not happy to have to submit a report that identified her as a member of an unhealthy triangle. She put the comment in because the intern insisted, and because several others had identified this particular triangle. The associate pastor had a strong stake in seeing this issue come up for discussion.

The triangle involving a congregation member, a staff member, and the pastor is one of the most familiar triangles known in church organizations. Pastors, unless they have a deep investment in controlling other people and having power over them, hate this particular triangle. It is important to break it up, and there is only one way to accomplish that: insist that a complaining member take the complaint to the staff member involved rather than bringing it to the pastor. That means, essentially, a flat, dogmatic refusal to participate in this triangle.

14. Careers

Some careers have a clear, expected pattern; others do not. Interns are expected to serve for eleven months. Although there is no denominational rule against it, an intern is expected *not* to serve on the staff after being ordained. This particular career is openly discussed, and everyone seems to understand it. One very popular intern four or five years ago really wanted to come back and was surprised to learn that, despite their affection for him, the congregation did not want him back as associate pastor.

Associate pastors are expected to stay four or five years but not longer. This may be an unacknowledged rule. Even though some people insist there is no such expectation, there has been no associate pastor who remained on the staff more than four years and ten months. Fifteen or sixteen years ago, one associate pastor who had been at the church three years was called as pastor when the pastor was killed in an accident. He had a happy and productive pastorate that lasted four more years.

Perhaps a normative career for associate pastors of this particular church ends by receiving a call to become pastor of a fairly large church. At least, that is what has happened here for as long as anyone can remember.

Looking back over the recent history of the church, we notice that no custodian has ever stayed at the church more than eighteen months. One move has already been made to dismiss the present custodian. Like successful attempts in the past, this move is unrelated to the quality of the custodian's work, which is uniformly judged to be superior. The request that the custodian be dismissed came from the Women's Association; our judgment is that this request came because the custodian insists that the Women's Association must make its requests for specific jobs through the pastor's office.

Comment. The comment about the custodian reveals a pattern in the life of the church that until this time had remained hidden. When this particular item came up in the report, the staff all agreed it was accurate, and the pastor decided to report it to the Council. His report created considerable anger and prompted a temporary split in the Council.

Apparently, there was once (and still may be) an unacknowledged rule that the custodian is accountable to the Women's Association. The pastor's action with the Council brought the rule out into the open.

15. Values

This question was hard to answer. At first we made a kind of nod in the direction of "Christian values," but then we had to admit that the question seems to get at some other things. We remembered the business of the attempt to fire the custodian, which suggested that fairness to employees was one of the values adhered to by the Church Council. But that in turn suggested that fairness to employees was *not* one of the values important to the Women's Association, which was an embarrassing thought. We then realized that it wouldn't be possible to avoid including some embarrassing material in this study, so we decided to include it.

We believe there may be some previously hidden value conflicts in the church as a whole. Some of these may be reflected in the staff, but we are not sure.

One matter having to do with values not reflected anywhere else in this study so far is our perception that the staff values individual, independent thought and effort. Evidence for this is that we cannot remember anyone at any time trying to limit anyone else's thinking or behavior, even when they were radically different from anyone else's.

We also suggest that the valuing of individuality and independence is reflected in the strong concern about office space previously discussed in this report.

Comment. This last paragraph suggests one of the values of this method. Although the questions may cover the same material over and over, sometimes coming at the staff interactions from one perspective will reveal material that none of the other approaches had uncovered.

16. Vulnerability

It would be relatively easy to disable staff operations in this church. All that would be necessary would be to undertake a remodeling program in the office areas and require staff to move their offices temporarily to the church parlor. (Someone has actually proposed this, by the way.) If everyone had to use the same space, even for as short a time as forty-eight hours, whatever underlying problems and difficulties exist would be brought to the surface very quickly. It would take weeks or months for the staff to recover from the impact of its loss of privacy.

Comment. The attack on the staff's functioning described briefly here is shrewd; it would probably work well. Consider a comparable situation. A major shift of operations in an agency of a large denomination a few years ago resulted in church employees moving to a new building in which no one except the four highest executives had a private office. One's rank was indicated by the height of the walls around one's work space. One executive who dealt with highly confidential material had no way of closing off access to her office and no way of preventing extremely sensitive conversations from being overheard by co-workers who had no business knowing the content of the discussions. The space arrangement was destructive of good functioning.

The compilers of the present study saw that a similar outcome could occur in their local setting. In fact, they saw such a space change as the quickest, most effective way to destroy relationships and effectiveness.

6

Two Cases in Brief

This chapter presents two cases in a briefer format, to let the reader see how a systems approach can provide a useful key to understanding what happens in a particular church staff.

THE SECRET RULES AT FISHER'S POINT

The Presbyterian Church of Fisher's Point had one thousand members.[1] Its staff supposedly comprised three ordained pastors, a business manager, and two secretaries. For some mysterious reason, it appeared difficult for the church to keep three ministers on the staff. Two of the ordained clergy had stayed for a number of years, but "third ministers" came and went with considerable regularity.

Everyone was puzzled. Pastor Smith and Associate Pastor Jones could not seem to construct a situation that would be satisfying to a third minister on the staff. Other than that, it was in most ways a thriving church. The resignations of ministers from that third position took place often enough that the presbytery took notice, and a committee found it necessary to conduct a quiet investigation, which turned up little if any information that could explain what was going on.

At first, it seemed as if the job description could bear

investigation. Two of the people who had resigned from the staff said they had felt terribly isolated dealing only with children and youth. But when job descriptions were rewritten so that Jones took major responsibility for youth work, and the new third minister had many of the responsibilities previously assigned to Jones, things were no better. Still later, the tasks of pastoral care and counseling had grown to such an extent that it seemed sensible to give the third minister responsibility for that area. Still another resignation. The case was reviewed and puzzled over for some time before an answer began to emerge.

That answer hinged upon the concept of written and unwritten rules. It was at a church officers' retreat that the notion of written and unwritten rules was brought up, and members of the Session and the Board of Deacons were invited to write down what they considered to be the basic rules by which the church operated.

The *written rules* at Fisher's Point Church included these:

1. Pastor Smith is the head of staff and Associate Pastor Jones is accountable to him.

2. Each staff member will have a job description that will place sharp boundaries around his or her functioning.

3. When a third minister is on the staff, it will be as the minister of pastoral care and counseling, and the job analysis will confine the minister to tasks appropriate to that role.

But someone put together a list of *unwritten rules* that looked something like this:

1. Smith and Jones will disregard job descriptions and will negotiate informally (that is, privately, with each other) about who does what. Each minister will actually perform all the tasks of ministry.

2. When there is a third minister, Smith and Jones will continue to do pastoral counseling.

3. When there is a third minister, he or she will *not* do any other tasks *except* pastoral counseling.

4. Smith and Jones are hereby named administrators of this agreement with full powers of enforcement.

Thus, the rules that everyone could see shaped the ministry in the church into two or perhaps three separate jobs. But the unwritten rules put restrictions on the third minister that were not binding upon the other two pastors.

Those unwritten rules, which also constituted a tacit contract, nailed a rigid triangle into place. I have already discussed rigid triangles as three-person systems in which one member of the triangle is perpetually isolated while the other two maintain a relationship that shuts the isolate out. That was the nature of the Fisher's Point setup. The rigid triangle practically ensured that no third minister would ever remain long on the staff of the church.

The obvious conclusion, given these observations, is that the church (or, at least, the staff) really could not make a place for a third minister. The staff (already consisting of at least four persons, two of whom formed an important subgroup) had no way to stop "triangling out" a new person.

This raises an intriguing question: Why did the staff believe that a third person was necessary? How did the repeated effort to secure a third pastor serve the system? It took a long time before the answer became clear. The truth was that the system did *not* need a third pastor; what it needed was *the myth that a third pastor was necessary.* What that myth did for the staff was to protect it from overwhelming demands on its time. It made the staff look so busy and overworked that members of the congregation were loath to ask anything more of their already overburdened ministers.

At the Fisher's Point Church, the relationship between

Smith and Jones can also be more clearly understood by reference to their roles. On the formal level, Smith was head of staff and Jones was accountable to him. Smith did the greater share of the preaching, and Jones behaved deferentially toward him when they appeared together in public. But on the informal level, Smith and Jones had a very different arrangement; they operated as friends, pastors, and equals. In practical terms that meant that except in cases of crisis, where a final, definitive decision had to be made quickly, the decisions from Smith had Jones's full approval and support and vice versa.

These arrangements were informal, not tacit; both men were perfectly able and willing to talk about them. But were there in fact any tacit roles? It is not clear that Smith had one. Jones did have a clear tacit role, however. It was to make sure that any third pastor knew it was impossible to break into the dyad.

Overall, the system was organized for effective work relationships. The team was highly effective and worked well with each other. It successfully maintained a vacant pastoral post as a symbol of how much work the pastors had to do and successfully defeated efforts to fill that post. Apparently, the team was able to fend off questions about why the post never stayed filled for long. That vacant third chair somehow ensured the survival and effectiveness of the team.

How might this situation be changed? Or should it be changed at all? The system worked well, so why tamper with it? The only problem is that there were several ministers whose lives may have suffered an unnecessary disruption by being employed at the church for such short periods.

In fact, the system never changed. Several more "third pastors," the last two of whom were women, served the Fisher's Point Church. Smith and Jones remained effective as pastors and were able to train and utilize every strong lay leadership. The two men retired within fifteen months of each other, and only then did the system go out of existence.

This case illustrates the fact that in many situations clear understanding does not necessarily produce change. Although a church officers' retreat managed to turn up the rules by which the staff actually operated, and even drew an accurate distinction between written and unwritten rules, or the openly acknowledged rules and the secret rules, nothing changed as a result of that discovery. The mere fact that we manage to discover what is actually going on in a situation does not mean changes will be made. Insight does not necessarily produce change.

What changes should or could have been made? To deal with the confusion and despair that were sometimes created for "third pastors" coming to Fisher's Point, the presbytery could have done what some presbyteries have in fact done in such situations: it could have required the church to close the third position permanently, to reconstruct its staffing plan to call for only two ordained pastors. That would have blown away the myth that a third minister was needed, the myth that Smith and Jones used to protect themselves from overly heavy demands on their time.

AN ANXIOUS TYRANT, AN ANGRY SABOTEUR (AND A SECRETARY)

The city fathers had predicted a rapid change in the community surrounding Meglin Memorial Church. A visitor five years ago could not help but be struck by the visible signs of deterioration in the neighborhood. So it is all the more striking to see Meglin Memorial Church today: a lively, vital place that survived considerable external turbulence and some quiet but determined infighting to become an exciting church. It is marked by traditional but lively worship, strong preaching, members of the congregation visibly involved in the community and the denomination, and warm and satisfying relationships both in the staff and in the congregation at large.

The pastor of the church when the community leaders were predicting deterioration was Dr. J. Salmon Baker. When the community was in the midst of all its changes, Dr. Baker could not fail to notice that members of the congregation were fleeing to the suburbs. Local denominational authorities were actively working at the development of new churches of the same denomination as Meglin Memorial in the three areas toward which members of the church were gravitating; the Committee on New Churches made a major effort to secure the cooperation of pastors closer in, asking them to name members who were moving, so that the missionary pastors in the new congregation might have a chance to find them. Many pastors cooperated, though with understandable reluctance. Baker did not. In fact, when his departed members began attending church in their new localities and asked for letters of transfer, he called on them, urging them to cancel the request, give up their interest in the new church, and return to Meglin Memorial. If they persisted, their request somehow "got lost" in the church office.

Baker insisted that Associate Pastor Albert Gruenschlager devote at least half time to an effort to keep people from moving their membership to one of the new churches. If a request for a letter of transfer went unanswered, Baker blamed Gruenschlager. The associate pastor responded angrily and began to undercut Pastor Baker in as many small ways as he could think of: such things as failing to attend important meetings and claiming that Baker had promised to attend them, or removing Baker's plans for the coming Sunday's worship from the desk of church secretary Elva Fitz.

The attrition took place anyway, and the church even began to consider closing its doors. A discouraged Baker retired after being censured by his denomination, and a last-ditch effort to revive the congregation was begun under the leadership of a new pastor, Woodward Harris.

Harris went to work vigorously in the neighborhood, encouraged people who had moved to the suburbs to find a new church where they lived, asked for Gruenschlager's resignation, got an experienced forty-two-year-old woman as his associate pastor, and developed as much lay leadership in the church as possible. In doing so, he had the support of a small group of four laypeople (one couple plus a remarkable seventy-two-year-old layman "itching for something to do") and an unusually competent and dedicated church secretary.

Here is a case demonstrating the need for changes in our understanding of what constitutes a multiple staff ministry. The church secretary who was of such help to the new pastor was the same church secretary—Elva Fitz—who had worked in the church when Baker and Gruenschlager were there. As long as Baker was the pastor, no one bothered to think of her as a member of the staff. Yet in fact it was her steadiness that helped the church not only to survive difficult changes but also to overcome the impact of Baker's overbearing style.

Any system is likely to have within it people whose behavior may express some of the system's needs but at the same time threaten the health of the system. When such people assume leadership positions, the threat to the system can be significant. Yet the system seems to survive, sometimes by the skin of its teeth. When that happens, you can sometimes discover someone who plays a powerful, hidden psychological role in the system. That's how it was with the Meglin Memorial Church. Miss Fitz used a secretary's traditional tools—telephone and typewriter—to encourage people, to soothe angry people, to recruit leadership. When Woody Harris arrived, she put on his desk a typed list with this heading: PEOPLE IN THIS CHURCH WHO HAVE SIGNIFICANT LEADERSHIP SKILLS BUT HAVE NEVER BEEN ASKED. A bemused pastor asked her for the source of the list, and Miss Fitz replied that she had found it on her desk and thought he might be interested in it. Of course she found it on her desk; she had put it there after she typed it. But she didn't say that.

If we look at the significant persons functioning in the church in the first place—Dr. Baker, Mr. Gruenschlager, *and* Miss Fitz—we can see something interesting if we take a systems point of view. Staffs and churches often nominate certain members to be the carriers of significant feelings or themes in the life of the system. The Meglin Memorial Church put its anxiety into Dr. Baker, its anger into Mr. Gruenschlager, and its determination to survive into Miss Fitz.

That may seem at first like an unnecessarily complex way to talk about the situation, but consider this. If the congregation did not have significant anxiety about the changing community, it probably would not have tolerated Baker's anxious behavior. Many people in the church knew about his attempts to get suburbanites to cancel their requests for letters of transfer, knew that such attempts were highly unethical, and attributed them to anxiety. And if it had not had a strong will to survive, Miss Fitz's own determination and diplomatic hard work would have been fruitless.

It may be a useful exercise for the reader to consider what a consultant might have done in the original situation to make the best use of Miss Fitz's strengths and to lessen the impact of Dr. Baker's anxious, unethical behavior.

7

The Anger Bearers:
A Consultation

In this chapter we meet the staff of the Church of All Saints in Uptontown and accompany a consultant in the early stages of his work with them. I have at points introduced fictional elements into the story to make sure the actual participants are not identifiable.

PRELIMINARY DATA

It will help to begin with a review of the way the polity of All Saints Church is supposed to work: the written rules.

The denomination of which the church is a part maintains the office of bishop.[1] Local congregations and bishops work together to identify potential clergy for the congregation. When a minister has been chosen by congregational vote, the bishop may confirm or refuse to confirm the choice. Except in certain time-limited situations, a bishop may not impose a minister upon a congregation; initiative always belongs with the congregation. It is understood that the relationship between a minister and a church is actually a three-party relationship, with the bishop as the third party.

Any of the three parties may end a pastoral relationship. The bishop may take initiative to dissolve a pastoral relationship. That step is taken only in unusual circumstances, and the bishop's authority is seldom used in this way; but if it is so used, the decision must be accepted.

(The congregation or the pastor can appeal to the Conference of Bishops, but that step is even more rarely taken.)
Minister or congregation may similarly take the initiative in
ending a pastoral relationship, and the bishop must accept
that decision. So a bishop may prevent a minister from
becoming one of the pastors in a particular congregation,
or may bring a pastoral relationship to an end, but may not
insist that a relationship be maintained if minister and/or
congregation want it ended.

In keeping with the ancient tradition that calls the bishop
the congregation's Visitor, bishops have the power to
investigate the life of a congregation.[2] In fact, that is how
this consultation began. Having received two strong communications, one from a member of the Church of All
Saints and one from an associate pastor, Bishop Ann
Westmark (the denomination's first woman bishop) decided to collect information about the church and its
pastoral staff.

All Saints was the largest church in the synod. Like many
large and influential churches—often called "tall steeple"
churches—in denominations with a presbyterian or episcopal polity, All Saints tended to operate as though it had a
congregational polity. The unspoken rule in the denomination was that the bishop's office would never interfere in
local church affairs and would always agree with the
congregation's choice of ministerial staff. For the bishop to
exercise her authority as Visitor was a rare action indeed.
Thus, when Pastor Allen Dircks and Congregational Clerk
Elwyn Davis received identical letters from Bishop
Westmark containing some pointed inquiries about staff
relationships in the church, each wrote her a very polite
response that told her without directly saying so that she
should mind her own business.

Bishop Westmark understood clearly the hidden meaning behind Dircks's and Davis's polite denials of any
difficulty and their suggestion that the congregation could
handle its own affairs adequately. But other discreet

telephoned inquiries convinced her that there was trouble brewing at All Saints Church, and she decided to proceed with an investigation.

Comment. We have not yet begun to discuss the actual staff situation at All Saints Church, but we already have information that we can consider from the point of view of the ideas in this book. One could of course also speculate on the forces operating within Pastor Dircks or Bishop Westmark or any other individuals involved. But these comments will be restricted to what can be seen from the particular perspective we have been using.

The thinking prevalent in the All Saints congregation and its staff, *and supported in the synod of which this congregation is a part,* is that bishops do not interfere in the life and work of large, influential churches. We should understand this as an unwritten rule. One of the first things our approach will then suggest is that, since it is unwritten, the rule is particularly powerful. It is impossible to imagine that the bishop is unaware of it. Her decision to exercise her powers of visitation is much more of a challenge than it might seem on casual inspection. Bishop Westmark is flinging down a gauntlet, and we may be sure that her action is understood that way at All Saints Church. Whatever the problems are (and whether or not the bishop's action is the best possible action to take under the circumstances), the stakes have been raised.

We might also conclude that merely by initiating an inquiry the bishop is already making some kind of change in the life of the congregation and the staff. Neither she nor we may be able to tell what that change is, but the bishop's inquiry has introduced a new element into All Saints, and that new element will reverberate throughout the system in ways that cannot quite be predicted. In some cases, merely making an inquiry or raising a question will bring about enough change to solve the problem. If the bishop is wise, she will wait to see what kinds of changes her questions alone may make before she takes any other kind of action. It is possible that Dircks and Davis may sit tight and hope that the difficulty—if there is a difficulty—will blow over. It is also possible that one or the other or both will take some kind of action inside the church. That action may solve the problem or result in increased damage.

THE BISHOP INQUIRES

Bishop Westmark waited to see if any changes might have taken place in Uptontown, but she heard little. Another complaint from a congregant, similar to the earlier complaint, arrived in a letter. The bishop decided to notify Pastor Dircks and Mr. Davis that she would attend the next regularly scheduled meeting of the Church Council. The Council was the governing body of the church, a group of twelve men and women with broad authority. When the Council met, the church staff would ordinarily be present.

At All Saints Church, the staff consisted of the following people: Allen Dircks was pastor and head of staff; Alice Denham and Frank Ferris were associate pastors; J. Theodore Atwood was minister of music; Min Jones and Denise Verbarg were the church secretaries. Mr. Atwood was a professional musician who also taught voice at the Traitt School of Music. There was also a church organist, Ardith Tenz, who was not considered a member of the church staff. The ordained ministers attended Council meetings; Min Jones did too, as a kind of assistant to Clerk Elwyn Davis. None of the rest of the staff attended Council meetings.

Although the staff encompassed all these people in one way or another, including even those who were not officially considered a part of the staff, the difficulty in the church seemed to have largely to do with two of the three ordained ministers.

Allen Dircks had been a widower for three years. His

wife and two of his three children had been killed in an automobile accident. At the time of the accident, the people of the church had rallied around him, but he had a hard time letting anyone minister to him. Now his surviving child, eighteen-year-old Linda, was a sophomore in college four hundred miles away. He had the reputation of being a hard worker and had not taken a vacation in three years.

Alice Denham was in her late thirties, the mother of two boys ages ten and twelve. Her husband, Ned, was the pastor of a church in Wellsville, about thirty-five miles from Uptontown. The Denhams lived in Wellsville, and Alice commuted to Uptontown to work at All Saints.

Frank Ferris, graduated from seminary two years ago, was twenty-seven. He was an accomplished musician, but his musical ideas were sharply different from those of J. Theodore Atwood. Frank was careful about where and when he performed, so as not to threaten the minister of music, who in Frank's eyes was pompous and overly sensitive. Marlys, Frank's wife, was carrying their first child but still working as a bank teller at the time of the consultation.

The bishop decided that her inquiry would be as brief and nonconfrontive as possible. What she hoped to do was find out enough to tell her whether the situation warranted stronger intervention of some kind. If it did, she planned to send in a professional consultant who would work only with the church and its staff and would not report to her. That way, she would establish her authority to make inquiry as to the "ecclesiastical health and spiritual welfare of the church," as the Book of Canons put it, and at the same time establish herself as helpful without being too intrusive.

People told Bishop Westmark that the problem centered around the troubled relationship between Allen Dircks and Alice Denham. Unable by church rules to fire Alice himself, the pastor had tried, it was said, to arouse sentiment in the congregation for her dismissal. But Alice had strong supporters in the church, and battle lines seemed to be forming.

When she arrived for her visitation, the bishop asked that the pastors meet individually with her and that the Council meet with her without the pastors present. In her conversations she made some discoveries.

Some people called the problem merely a clash of personalities. Others, however, pointed out that Alice, a mother of young children and a strong-minded and capable woman, managed her time carefully, limiting the hours she spent at All Saints to those contracted for. Allen Dircks, who began to appear more and more like a workaholic,[3] was highly dissatisfied with Alice's insistence on sticking to her contract. Several times he had asked her to do something, and she had said she could not or would not. Dircks, who said he worked a ninety-hour week— which some called boasting, and others complaining— was open in his criticism of a woman who was only willing to work "fifty hours a week." There was a sense in which the situation could be called a clash of personalities, but that was too bland and unrevealing a way to put it. By the time the bishop was making her inquiries, Mr. Dircks was openly referring to Mrs. Denham (Alice hated the designation *Ms.*) as lazy and eager to find ways to avoid work. Alice Denham was refusing to respond openly to these criticisms and would not defend herself, according to some of her frustrated supporters.

On the basis of her visit, the bishop decided to engage a consultant to work with All Saints Church. She conferred with Allen Dircks and with several lay leaders, including some of Alice Denham's supporters; she did not speak to anyone else on the staff about her plans. At district expense, she engaged the services of Valley Pastoral Associates, a corporation that performed a variety of services for local churches. VPA appointed Jonas Kendall to serve as consultant.

Comment. In many ways this situation appears to be a personal conflict between a pastor and an associate pastor. Both people may be seen in positive or negative terms, depending on the observer's background and opinions.

Taking a systems-oriented view of the situation will mean looking for the systems meaning of almost every feature of this situation, including the pastor's style and work habits, the associate pastor's style and work habits, the nature of the conflict between them, the willingness of Pastor Dircks to make his complaints public, the *un*willingness of Associate Pastor Denham to do the same, and, most of all, the functions that all these behaviors perform for the staff and the congregation.

Note how many overlapping groups are involved in this staff situation.

There is the district. Its chief operating officer is a bishop deeply concerned about a congregation within the district, and determined to use her episcopal powers to erase the difficulties. In some settings, powers seem to exist for the purpose not of actual use but of potential use. One wonders if that is the case here, and if the bishop may have been more heavy-handed than she realizes. If so, it may be that the rules, written and unwritten, make any action a bishop takes heavy-handed; no amount of delicacy on Bishop Westmark's part will actually come across as delicate.

There is the All Saints congregation. The consultant is assigned to be of help to the congregation *and* the staff, but there's a sense in which he has been imposed on the congregation. That poses some problems for him of forming a working alliance with members and staff of All Saints.

There is the staff itself: we know very little about it, except that two of its members seem to be at odds. And yet that is the situation on which we are eventually to focus.

THE CONSULTANT AT WORK

Jonas Kendall's way of beginning was to review the information he already had, raising in his own mind a series of questions. Here are some of the questions he raised as he reviewed the material from All Saints:

1. Of what value to the staff is Allen Dircks's workaholic pattern?
2. Of what value to the staff is Alice Denham's carefully managed and limited schedule?
3. Of what value to the staff is the clash between the two?
4. Of what value are these things to the congregation?
5. In what other ways can I understand the meanings of these patterns? How else can I describe or label them? How do the new labels expand the answers to my earlier questions?
6. What meaning does the conflict between pastor and associate pastor have for the rest of the staff? For the congregation?

Given what he had been told, he began to think that Alice Denham had a strong sense of boundaries, while Allen Dircks did not. (What value did the pastor's lack of a sense of boundaries and the associate's strong sense of boundaries have for the staff? For the congregation?)

More than anything else, Kendall wanted to work with the whole staff. The hot spot seemed to be there. It was also important to him to have the staff see him as their ally rather than as a dangerous outsider. He asked Pastor Dircks to hold a staff meeting at which he, as consultant, would work with them. As he looked around the group, Kendall tried to discern who among them might be experiencing the least amount of conflict yet be fairly near the center of what was going on. He finally chose Frank Ferris.

Kendall made use of a powerful tool called *sculpting*. He began by asking Frank to think of the members of the group as materials in a "sculpture," and to pose Allen and

Alice in a way which to Frank depicted the way they characteristically related to each other. Frank posed them facing each other about two feet apart, bent over with hands on knees; the impression somewhat resembled linemen on opposing football teams. Frank then was to put the rest of the staff into the sculpture, adding himself last.

Frank's final version of the sculpture was interesting; he had everybody else standing around Allen and Alice in a circle, watching.

"How does it feel to be in that position, Allen?" asked Jonas Kendall.

"Weird," answered the pastor. "It feels like a scene from one of those old movies about school kids, where two guys go to a vacant lot to have it out, and everybody else goes along to watch. There's an immature, adolescent quality to it."

"Alice?"

"It's almost embarrassing. I get the feeling—maybe it's like Allen's boxing match—that the two of us are putting on some kind of a show for the rest of the staff."

"Anybody else have a comment?"

"I think it's very accurate, what they're saying," said Denise Verbarg. "All of us do sit around wondering how the anger between Pastor Dircks and Pastor Denham is going to erupt next."

J. Theodore Atwood said something under his breath.

"Mr. Atwood?"

"What I said was, 'Speak for yourself.' I for one do not sit around waiting to see these two fight."

"Well, you've really helped us, Frank," said Jonas Kendall. "And so have the two of you," he said, nodding toward Denise Verbarg and Theodore Atwood.

"Have we really?"

"Yes. You've helped us see one of the patterns in the staff. The staff has gotten Pastor Dircks and Pastor Denham to do your fighting for you."

"*For* us?"

"Yes. This group comes across as angry, but you also

seem like a group that has a hard time actually being as angry as you feel. So you've elected these two to be angry with each other. They aren't actually the only angry ones around here, and Frank has told us that with his sculpture."

"Oh, I don't think that's true," said Min Jones.

"Yes, it is," said Alice and Allen almost in the same breath.

Everybody stared at them.

Alice looked around the room angrily. "Of course Allen and I disagree about managing time. I think he's a workaholic, and he thinks I'm lazy. I don't like his carelessness about worship. I don't like the theology or lack of it behind his worship. And he doesn't like mine. But we also respect each other's strengths, and in many ways we get along reasonably well. But you all have made a show out of our disagreements, pretending that we're the only angry ones and that anger is the only feeling we have toward each other. In the immortal words of Colonel Sherman Potter, horse hocky!"

"Do you have a suggestion, Mr. Kendall?" asked Allen Dircks. It was hard to tell whether his question was serious or sarcastic, but he went on. "I'm embarrassed and angry now, and I want that right out in the open. Until we went through this exercise, it never occurred to me that Alice and I were practically putting on a show for you. I don't like it, and I want it changed, and that's why I want suggestions from you."

Comment. One significant aspect of the problem has been uncovered, but it is by no means solved. A lot of hard work lies ahead both for the staff and for the consultant. But more has already been accomplished than anyone expected.

We will not have space in this book to discuss sculpting fully. It is a powerful tool, because it can so often get behind all our rational, wordy ways of understanding things and reveal to us the feeling life that lies underneath the surface. On the other hand, there is no guarantee that sculpting will work as well (or as quickly) in every case as it did in this one, and sometimes people experience it as rather threatening. There are some cautions to be observed in its use; like all tools that have power, it can be misused. But in this case, Jonas Kendall's introduction of sculpting broke through a great deal of defense quickly and without excessive pain.[4]

Only one interpretation was necessary. Like many good interpretations, it took in a great deal of territory. What Kendall saw in the sculpture was two staff members cast as the "Angry Ones." Alice Denham and Allen Dircks had been nominated (because they did have a strong and somewhat angry disagreement with each other) to roles as angry people.

A THEOLOGICAL PARENTHESIS

Anger appears to pose a theological problem for many Christians. We find ourselves engaging in many other behaviors that function to hide anger or to maintain a pretense that we don't have it. Not long ago, the director of a pastoral counseling center asked the center's staff for feedback concerning the strengths and weaknesses of the center's operation. A relatively new staff member said the unspeakable by pointing out that a major weakness was the center's insistence on operating on a conflict-avoidance model. "We might do better," said the new counselor, "if we had a couple of good 'mads.'" One would expect pastoral counselors to have considerable expertise in helping people make constructive use of their anger rather than denying it or using it destructively, and that was true of this staff. But *in its own operations* it was a group unwilling to express its own anger.

In the case of All Saints Church, Alice Denham finally broke out into open anger with the rest of the staff, ending it with a quotation from a character on the television program *M*A*S*H*, one designed to stand for a stronger expletive. Even though Alice couched her own anger in somewhat humorous terms and avoided saying any words unacceptable in themselves, Min Jones was offended. She never quite forgave Alice for the quotation from Colonel Potter.[5]

Min's attitude is common; open expression of anger is unacceptable, and the more power it has, the less acceptable it becomes. Only slightly hidden behind Min's overt opinion ("You shouldn't say such things") is a very destructive stance ("You shouldn't *feel* that way").

It is clear that anger simply *is*, and any effort to deny its existence, or to tell ourselves that we should not feel it, is not just a mistake but a misperception and a denial of our nature before God. Elsewhere, Herbert Anderson and I have written:

> There are two seemingly opposite but deeply related ways of mishandling anger. . . . We can dwell on the anger, nurse it along, let it become the major preoccupation of the mind. Or we can refuse to consider anger, refuse to recognize it when it emerges, reject it as abnormal. In either case, [we are] being dominated by anger.[6]

In a system that as a whole is having such difficulty with anger, one of the most common solutions to the problem is to elect members of the system to be the angry people in the system. The language is in part figurative, to be sure. The members of the system may not realize that there is a problem and do not think of what they are doing as a solution, and of course no election is held; I have made that clear in earlier chapters. Yet the language is legitimate. "Problem" and "solution" and "election" may not be literally accurate words, but they describe what is taking place.

Those who make the study of group behavior a specialty sometimes use slightly different language; they refer to behavior that occurs in a group and knowledge that exists in a group as the "property of the group." In conferences designed for the study of group behavior, a consultant may point out to a group seeming to lack crucial information that the information does exist in the group. The consultant is referring to the fact that at least one member of the group actually has the information, although it is not currently being shared. (Other group members often become angry at this point.) Similarly, behavior a group could prevent, but does not, is behavior belonging to the group, and the entire group bears the responsibility for it. Naturally enough, group members don't want to take that responsibility and often become angry when this truth is pointed out to them.[7] In such a situation, one group member ruefully remarked, "I've heard a proverb that says 'In the kingdom of the blind the one-eyed man is king.' It isn't true. In the kingdom of the blind the one-eyed man is a @ #) (&&!! troublemaker."

The struggle between Pastor Dircks and Associate Pastor Denham is the *whole staff's behavior*, because to this point the staff as a group has tolerated it and made no effective effort to stop it. One wonders if Luke was not getting at the same thing in the story of Stephen's martyrdom: "And Saul was consenting to his death" (Acts 8:1).

When Christian groups have difficulty with anger, as they often do, one of the things they are most likely to do is to "put the anger into" some of their members. The group can then condemn the angry expressions but is unlikely to do so in ways that will actually bring an end to the behavior. Such group behavior satisfies both the need to be angry and the need to condemn anger. Observations from an outsider that this is what is happening may well be pooh-poohed. But catching the group in the act and commenting upon what one sees is sometimes effective. Anger is, of course, not the only emotion dealt with this way.

Such information is valuable to anyone working with a staff. If a particular person—or, as happened in the case we are studying, a pair of people—engages in behavior that seems to embarrass others or draw expressions of distaste and disapprobation, it's useful to assume that such behavior is expressing a need of the group. The misbehaver, like the scapegoated child in a family, is performing a function on the group's behalf.

THE CONSULTANT INTERVENES

The sculpting exercise had ended with Alice Denham's angry speech and Allen Dircks's request for a suggestion from Jonas Kendall.

"Our time today is almost up, and, yes, I do have a suggestion for the group," Kendall said. "I would like each of you to put down on paper your greatest dissatisfaction about the way this staff operates. Pastor Dircks, I would like to enlist your authority as head of staff here to see that each person completes that assignment. When each of you has written your greatest dissatisfaction down, I'd like you to give it, unsigned, to Mrs. Denham. Meanwhile, I'm going to ask you to *make no changes* in your present way of operation."

Slightly baffled but interested, the staff nodded assent as Jonas Kendall looked around at each face.

Comment. If we look back to the beginning of this story, we may be able to notice that things have come rather a long way. Almost everyone involved, including perhaps even the bishop, perceived "the problem" as being some kind of interpersonal clash between Alice Denham and Allen Dircks. By now it should appear that this is not the case.

This does not mean, however, that there is no clash between the pastor and the associate pastor; there is a clash, and the clash is a problem. It may in fact be a very serious problem, with the potential for significantly under-cutting the ministry in All Saints Church. But by now we are in a position to see that the problem between Pastor Dircks and Associate Pastor Denham is symptomatic of a problem that is more subtle, more hidden, and more pervasive.

The consultant's assignment for the group had several purposes all at once. First, it affirmed the authority of the pastor as head of staff. When a consultant is called in, there is always some danger that the consultant will take over and undercut the authority of the person who ordinarily has responsibility for directing an operation. Good systems consultants remember this, and they remember to affirm the authority of those who ordinarily have it in a system.[8]

Second, Kendall also affirmed the authority of the associate pastor. Such authority may be less than that of the pastor; in fact, if it is equal to or greater than the pastor's, the system is already in trouble. But the system is also in trouble if the authority of an associate pastor is nonexistent or if people do not recognize it.

The third thing Kendall did was to assume the existence of dissatisfactions. Whenever there exists a situation in which one is likely to encounter denial of negative perceptions or opinions, it is particularly useful to try to cut such denials off at the pass. In premarital counseling, it is not particularly useful to ask couples if they've had a fight yet or if they think they are going to have fights, but it is very useful to ask them what they think their first fight will be about. Kendall was operating on the same principle when he asked each staff member to write down the single greatest dissatisfaction. He assumed the dissatisfactions and asked the staff to differentiate between them. This may not completely bypass the denial, but it clearly suggests that dissatisfactions are normal. If anyone at the next meeting does deny that there is any dissatisfaction, others from the staff will be more likely to challenge the denial.

Finally, Kendall asked the staff to make no changes in its present mode of operation. Such an injunction has several effects, but in order to understand them, we need to explore the possible responses. There are two: resistance and compliance. The consultant has to take both possibilities into account. Consider at the same time the fact that changes in the staff's operation are part of the long-range goal toward which the staff hopes to move.

Resistance often takes place in order not to comply: that is, in order not to yield to the authority of the consultant. But if the staff resists Kendall's injunction not to change anything, it can only do so by changing something—which is the whole point of having a consultant in the first place. To resist this particular injunction is to move toward the goal on which staff and consultant are working: that is, to comply.

Obviously, to comply is to yield authority to Kendall so he can help move the staff toward change.

What Kendall has done, in fact, is to create what is called in clinical circles a "therapeutic double bind." If the staff complies, Kendall wins—but so do they, because they are creating the conditions for change. If the staff resists, Kendall wins—but so do they, because they are already moving toward change.

In the meantime, there are some other meanings to the injunction. Suppose the staff feels paralyzed, unable to do anything and particularly unable to make any changes. By suggesting that they not make any changes, Kendall raises in a subtle way the possibility of change. If *he* warns them against making changes, it must mean he believes they could make some changes if they tried.

A LATER MEETING

We can stay with this consultation for only one more round, although the relationship actually lasted for six months. The next step the staff and the consultant took together, however, made a significant change in the staff's operation and in the church's life. It came directly out of Jonas Kendall's assignment that each person write down on paper one single greatest dissatisfaction.

Min Jones wrote: "I don't like all the anger that's always flying all over the place all the time."

Alice Denham wrote: "When I am to preach, it is my

authority and my responsibility to construct the liturgy: choose the hymns, write out the texts of the unison prayers, and other such things. It infuriates me that Allen often changes the hymns I have chosen and rewrites some of the prayers. I try to use nonsexist language in the prayers, and when they are printed in the bulletin, the same old sexist language has been put back in. I wonder why I have never let anyone know how angry I am about that until now."

Allen Dircks wrote: "It galls me that Alice Denham is not as invested in the life of this church as I am. But what galls me even more is that she keeps blaming me for things that are not my fault."

But no one knew what anyone else had written. Kendall had asked that everyone give the sheets of paper with the dissatisfactions written on them to Alice Denham. At the next meeting he had with the staff, he asked Alice if she had them with her, and she said she did.

"Can you identify who wrote each one?" asked Kendall.

"I think so. This one's Denise's, and—"

"No, please don't tell us now. I would like to spend some time today seeing how well you really communicate with each other. Pastor Dircks, what would you suppose is the biggest complaint Denise Verbarg has?"

"Ah . . . probably the heavy load she carries of running the machines. Some days she never gets out of what we call the Print Shop."

"What's your guess, Mrs. Jones?"

"Oh, I think pastor is right. Poor Denise is sometimes so isolated."

Kendall went around the room, asking each person what they supposed was the least satisfactory thing about Denise's job. And then he asked Alice to give Denise her own paper back.

"Now, Denise," said Kendall, "would you be willing to read what you've written?"

Denise smiled as she began to read from her paper. " 'It's very difficult to work in the Print Shop when people keep coming in with last-minute changes, particularly on the worship bulletin.' " She looked around the group. "You see, it's not the isolation; it's the confusion."

"Can you say more about the confusion? I don't understand." It was Pastor Dircks speaking, and Kendall did not intervene.

"Well, like I get the bulletin typed and ready to run, and then somebody comes in and tells me the hymn numbers have been changed."

"Changed?" Alice Denham asked.

"Well, yes, Alice, particularly when it's your worship service."

"Allen, why do you change my hymn choices? Mr. Kendall, may I read my complaint?" Alice did not wait for Kendall to respond, but read the complaint we have already heard.

"Alice," said Allen Dircks, "*I* don't change your hymn choices."

"Come on, Allen, if you don't, who does?"

A tense silence enveloped the whole group. Finally, two voices spoke at the same time: "I do." And then the speakers, Min Jones and Theodore Atwood, looked at each other.

Min went on. "Well, Mrs. Denham tends to pick very modern hymns, and sometimes she gives us new texts for the old hymns and wants the new text printed in the bulletin. It makes the bulletin too long, and I know that what she wants to sing doesn't reflect this congregation's way of thinking. So sometimes I've asked Mr. Atwood to suggest a different hymn. After all . . ."

"It seems clear that we're not going to complete the reading of the papers today," said Jonas Kendall. "We'll get to all of them eventually. But right now it looks as if a kind of secret has been uncovered. Mrs. Denham, I gather that you've been supposing that the pastor has been changing your hymn selections, and perhaps you're surprised that it was not the pastor at all."

"Yes, I am surprised, and I'm even angrier than I was. Min, you had no right—"

Min Jones grew angry too. "Well, you never said a word, so I assumed you didn't object. After all, I've been secretary here for twenty-five years, and I know this congregation better than anyone else."

It had never occurred to Alice Denham that remaining silent about her dissatisfaction contributed to maintaining the pattern about which she was so angry.

Before the conversation had gone much farther, the pastor stepped in with his own authority.

"Just let's get this clear. When I construct the worship service, no one is to change anything in it without my approval. Understood? And when Alice constructs the worship service, no one is to change anything in it without *her* approval. Don't even correct our grammar or spelling; if you have a question, just call it to my attention or to Alice's. Understood? And if she and I have disagreements about what goes in the bulletin, we will hash that out between the two of us. Understood?"

Comment. We are about to let the staff of All Saints Church solve the rest of their problems themselves. Meanwhile, however, the consultant's interventions have made a great deal of difference already.

Perhaps the most powerful intervention was the rather dramatic uncovering of a secret in the life of the staff: Min Jones, with the collusion of J. Theodore Atwood, had been changing Alice Denham's worship materials, undermining Alice's authority, and keeping Alice's anger with Allen Dircks at the boiling point. But she had another ally in the process: Alice herself, who by keeping this particular aspect of her anger to herself had invited Min to go on with what she was doing.

Why did Jonas Kendall have the slips written, given to Alice, and given back to their authors after the staff had speculated on what other staff members had written? We do not know exactly why. Nor can we be sure that it was the most effective or wise intervention he could have used.

We can surmise, however, that Kendall meant what he said when he told the staff, "I would like to spend some time today seeing how well you really communicate with each other." He was already aware that there was a conflict-avoidance model operating in the staff, and thus he had to have known that communication was inadequate or emotionally dishonest or both. It was likely that the revealing of sentiments that ordinarily had been kept private would bring to light some kind of secret, the exposure of which would exercise considerable power.

We also need to say that Kendall had no way to predict whether that exposure and that power would have a beneficial effect. He had to rely on the assumption that, in general, the power of secret-keeping is destructive and the power of exposure is healing. That is, in fact, one meaning of the biblical dictum that "the truth shall set you free."

It is helpful to notice that when Allen Dircks took over the meeting with some forcefully stated instructions—note the repeated and angry use of the word "understood"—Kendall did not take back control of the meeting. This was the pastor using his authority in a clear, unambiguous, constructive way. What Dircks was doing was supportive both of his own authority and that of his associate pastor.

In the long run, Alice Denham remained on the staff at All Saints for the next three years. Her relationship with Allen Dircks was marked with open conflict from time to time, but they developed deep respect and even affection for each other. Min Jones offered her resignation and Allen Dircks refused to accept it, insisting that Min's value to the life of the congregation was very great indeed.

And the bishop has not visited All Saints since

8

Principles

So far we have discussed the ways in which paying attention to how churches and staffs work can provide ways to improve their functioning. In this chapter I want to suggest principles that can be used to gauge the health of a multiple ministry situation. They can be used as a kind of guide for a staff or team to test itself, at least in a rough-and-ready way. To a lesser extent, these principles suggest some things that can be done to help groups in trouble, but I have already pointed to those in earlier chapters.

Two forces always balance each other in the life of any working group: the need to maintain itself, to cohere, to survive; and the need to get work done, to function effectively. Often enough these two forces work together, but sometimes putting time and energy into keeping the group going takes time and energy away from doing its work.

Years ago I suggested five Principles of Coherence and five Principles of Effective Functioning.[1] Those two categories still make sense, even if some of the principles now look a bit different.

PRINCIPLES OF COHERENCE

A ministering staff will be more likely to remain together and create for itself a more stable environment to the extent that:

1. Every time a staff member is added or subtracted, the staff examines and defines the whole ministry it is called to carry out, in and for the congregation, and redivides the responsibilities

2. Open and free communication between the staff members is encouraged

3. Negative aspects of staff relationships are appropriately and openly dealt with

4. The nature of each individual's contribution to the ministry of the whole group is accurately described

5. Reliable information about activities, problems, and plans is consistently and regularly available throughout the system

Let us look a little more closely at these five principles.

1. Every time a staff member is added or subtracted, the staff examines and defines the whole ministry it is called to carry out, in and for the congregation, and redivides the responsibilities. If my experience in workshops over the last twenty years is any guide, I would expect this principle to run into more resistance than any other. If taken seriously, it is very demanding. I have often referred to it as "describing and reslicing the pie." It is no small matter for a responsible working group of people to try to describe everything they are attempting to do on behalf of those they serve. The first time this exercise is undertaken, it may require a whole day's work, or even more. (Subsequent repeats are easier and less time-consuming.)

I am deeply indebted to the staffs with whom I have worked in the last two decades. From many staffs who use this model, I have learned that it is indeed a process of great importance and can make a strong contribution to the coherence of a staff. Some groups, however, have made it plain that they cannot carry on a program of this kind. Their work load is too heavy, the demands on their time too imperative. "It is no doubt a useful idea," they say, "but you cannot expect our staff to undertake it. It would be too much."

I respect those staffs who point out what a demand this process makes, and from them I have learned a great deal about the realities of some staff situations. But in consulting with multiple staffs, I always looked for factors that may be of unusual importance, and this turns out to be one of them. It is of course far more time-consuming to carry out than one might like. Regularly—that is, at least once a year and certainly each time there is a change in personnel —the staff (preferably in the presence of lay representatives) defines the *total* ministry for which it is responsible. When that total ministry is defined, the staff then decides how (and by whom) that total ministry is to be carried out. This repeated review of "what does the whole pie look like and how is it to be divided?" is, I am convinced, utterly essential.

Whenever a staff member leaves, the tasks that person was carrying do not disappear; they are still a part of the total ministry expected or required of the staff. When a staff examines its overall ministry, it is forced to examine those tasks and to make provision for carrying them out. Perhaps they will be assigned to one of the other staff members; perhaps they will be reassigned to a lay person in the congregation; perhaps the staff will need to make clear to the congregation that in the absence of the departed staff member they will not be carried out at all. But *some* provision must be made.

When a new staff member comes on the scene, a similar process must take place: redefining the tasks of the staff in the light of this new addition. This process is, frankly, far more important than drawing up a job description. Job descriptions offer a very deceptive security; there's a cliché that says they always become lies the day after they are drawn up. This is essentially accurate; that's why it became a cliché.

A job description is a protective document; aside from its original devising, it is almost never used except to say "You're not doing your job" or "You're asking me to do work you have no right to expect." Sometimes that's necessary; members of a team need to know what they can expect of each other. More than that, however, they need to know it in the context of what the team as a whole is trying to accomplish. Very little changes when a team tries to do without formal job descriptions. An amazing amount changes when it tries to operate without a clear picture of its overall task and how each person fits into that task.

2. Open and free communication between the staff members is encouraged. This principle is an important factor in the stability and coherence of a staff. There is hardly anything so powerfully destructive in a system as the shutting down of communication or the development and maintenance of secrets. In some systems, such as families, the forces holding the family together are so powerful that the maintenance of secrets distorts the family and damages the persons and relationships within it, but may not actually destroy the family. In a work system, however (such as a multiple staff), the system itself may be destroyed; the forces holding it together are not so powerful as those within a family.

Two recent events have brought the relevance of this principle powerfully to my mind. "Event" may not be exactly the right word for the first; I have just finished reading Pat Conroy's powerful novel *The Prince of Tides*[2] and recommend it to anyone wanting to understand more richly how families operate and how secrets are destructive. Second, a church staff situation with which I am acquainted has come into grave danger because judicatory officials have encouraged various boards and committees in a local church to keep secrets from the pastor and have then told the pastor that such secrets exist and are being kept from him. It is hard to imagine a more effective prescription for disaster.

3. *Negative aspects of staff relationships are appropriately and openly dealt with.* When negative aspects of a situation are denied awareness, they do not disappear, but remain as sources of resentment and potential hostility. In any system, there is dangerous pretense in the bland denial that failures have taken place or that hostile feelings exist.

Nor can there be much doubt that this principle has to do with the coherence and stability of the group. I have recently had the opportunity to observe the workings of a church staff consisting of three ordained persons, a secretary, and about twelve part-time volunteers, all of whom receive a great deal of recognition from the pastor, and all of whom began their service with a strong investment in the church and its programs. In the group, several strong personalities have come and gone in the relatively short time I have had an opportunity to observe. Positive achievements and accomplishments receive the recognition they deserve. But what also happens repeatedly is that negative events—disagreements, programs that don't quite come off, mix-ups, and other relatively minor problems—are all swept under the rug. "Seldom is heard a discouraging word," but as a consequence the morale of the group is low, and volunteers who begin with strong and deep commitments stop making their contributions and pull out. The church's operating staff has little or no stability.

4. *The nature of each individual's contribution to the ministry of the whole group is accurately described.* At first, I thought that what was important was that the nature of people's contributions be *recognized.* And I don't really deny that. Those who work with family systems quickly learn that each individual in the family has an identifiable role, although the family may have some kind of invest-

ment in not recognizing that role. If the family in fact fails to recognize the role, the effective functioning of the family may be compromised, to say nothing of the difficulties the person carrying the role may experience.

The theological aspect of this principle is that it flows from a sense of the worth of the individual before God.

I have learned, however, that recognizing the value of each individual's contribution does not in itself contribute much to the stability and coherence of the team. There is an amazingly large number of people who either do not need recognition of that sort or do not want it. People do need to feel as thought they and their work are valued, and when they do not get that feeling they may become less effective; but that contributes less to incoherence and instability in the staff than one might think. (It may contribute to a lack of productivity.)

The principle should read that "a multiple staff will tend to remain more stable and coherent if the nature of each individual's contribution to the ministry of the whole group is *accurately described*." Having one's work *valued* contributes to one's own productivity; having one's work *accurately described* contributes to the whole group's stability and coherence.

This may come across more clearly if we examine the opposite case. There are few ways to destabilize a system more effectively than to create overlapping and conflicting responsibilities, to proclaim that a certain member of the team is doing Job A when in fact that person is doing Job B, to make it difficult for a new person to discover where keys (or supplies, or authority, or any other tool needed for his or her work) are to be found. Sometimes a system will effectively protect itself from outsiders for a while by developing a secret list of people's responsibilities while publicly giving out a very different list. But that device comes with a time bomb; eventually a system using it will collapse in disorder.

5. *Reliable information about activities, problems, and*

plans is consistently and regularly available throughout the system. Not long ago I talked with a man on a large judicatory staff. All told, there were twelve staff members: a bishop, a diocesan administrator (the man I was talking with, a clergyman), four other ordained ministers, a treasurer, a summer program director, and four secretaries. The group consisted of seven women and five men. The diocesan administrator was asking, in a bitter tone, why he should remain in his job; he seemed utterly demoralized.

"The bishop is a man with wonderful visions and creative imagination," he said, "but he simply cannot bring himself to communicate with the rest of us. In the last three months he's done a whole series of things that have devastated staff morale. He took a whole set of responsibilities away from Pamela and gave them to Henry."

The third man at the table chimed in. "Well, he *is* the bishop, isn't he?"

"Not the point. Of course he's the bishop. But he arranged the whole new system with Henry without consulting or telling anyone. Not anyone! Pamela didn't know her job had been changed until she asked Laurie to type a letter for her about something, and Laurie had to tell her it wasn't her bailiwick any more. And what he's done to the camp and conference committee!"

"Hm?" said the two of us listening.

"Well, Jim is a terrific summer program administrator, but he does tend to be an empire builder. He went privately to the bishop and got him to commit the diocese to a whole new program that the camp and conference committee has turned down four times—and the bishop was at those meetings and voted to turn the program down too. There are nine people on that committee—I should say there *were* nine people. Six of them resigned last week, in a joint letter, in which they told the bishop that if he was going to make all the decisions without even informing them, they didn't see any need for a committee. The bishop was nonplussed!"

The conversation continued in this vein for some time.

Information is obviously not consistently and reliably available in this system, and the system is paying the price. Valuable committee members have resigned their posts, and four of the twelve staff members are actively seeking other employment. For a while they kept their job searches quiet, but word has gotten out. The bishop seems genuinely unclear about why his staff is disappearing out from under him.

In this particular case, the reason why information is not regular and reliable in the system is that its leader operates as a Lone Ranger. He actually has little sense of teamwork. (All his previous responsibilities called on him for a solo performance.) The system cannot tolerate the style this individualistic newcomer has brought. In many instances, however, an entire system will develop a pattern of life in which surprises are often sprung on members in a similar way. Such a system will not be very stable, but it could absorb a bishop of this kind because its style is similar to his. He will know the unwritten rules of the system: "Don't let anyone know what you are going to do until you have done it." "It is dangerous to be too open." "Play your cards close to your chest."

Some years ago, the central offices of a large denomination underwent significant restructuring. Many changes were suddenly sprung on employees at all levels. A bitter one-line joke sprang up among the staff: "If my boss calls while I'm away from my desk, get his name." Even a casual observer could see familiar structures disintegrating and instability growing. A number of people familiar with management principles became convinced that the central administrative officers had chosen instability and wanted deliberately to create as much instability as possible; whether that was the case or not, instability was what was achieved.

PRINCIPLES OF EFFECTIVE FUNCTIONING

A multiple staff will tend to perform the functions of its ministry more adequately if:

1. The staff has clearly defined goals
2. The staff recognizes that the relationships it maintains within itself are models for the relationships in the congregation
3. The staff provides for the regular exercise by one or more of its members of all the necessary leadership functions
4. The staff has a broad consensus concerning the nature and purpose of the church and its ministry
5. Provision is made for authority, responsibility, and accountability

1. The staff has clearly defined goals. This principle needs only brief discussion. First, it treats the staff of a church as an organic unity. That's how systems thinking approaches a working group such as a staff. Second, a set of common goals, clearly defined and shared by the group, is essential to the effective accomplishment of the group's task.

2. The staff recognizes that the relationships it maintains within itself are models for the relationships in the congregation. When a subsystem takes leadership in a larger system, the smaller system's management of relationships is likely to be taken by members of the larger system as the norm for relationships. If that sounds too technical, remember that the way in which the significant adults (usually the parents, but including a single parent's way of relating to other adults) manage their relationships with each other in a family is usually what the children come to think of as the norm for adult relationships. The single most powerful factor in the way a man treats his wife is the way he saw his father treating his mother, *even when he now believes intellectually that it was not a good relationship.*

So it is in a congregation. The executive subsystem provides the most powerful single model for relationships throughout the system.

3. The staff provides for the regular exercise by one or more of its members of all the necessary leadership functions. Actually, what is important is that the provision for those functions be as conscious as possible. When it happens unconsciously, it still happens, but not under the control of members of the system. What a staff needs to have happen will usually happen. What is not so certain is that the members of the staff plan for it and take charge of it. The staff needs to know which leadership functions are being performed and by whom. Then questions can be raised that put the staff more firmly in control of its own processes.

4. The staff has a broad consensus concerning the nature and purpose of the church and its ministry. A staff that has reached a consensus about the nature of the church and its ministry will experience less intramural conflict than one that has not. The systems aspect of such an issue is not whether a team has consensus or not but the way in which consensus is reached.

We are drawn once again to the business of defining the total nature of the ministry a team is to carry out in and for a congregation. Of course, when a group tries to define its total ministry, there will be conflict, different ideas, different perceptions. What lies behind specific differences about tasks will often be a general difference in vision about the nature of church and ministry. That is exactly the place where the pie-describing and pie-slicing exercise begins: with all the differences in ideas and perceptions out on the table for debate and decision.

"What in the name of the Lord are we about?" That is the question that has to be hammered at, wrestled with, debated, and worked on time and again. It is not particularly hard to decide that the person hired for her administrative skills will be assigned many administrative tasks, or that the one with strong interest in Christian education will carry out a large share of the ministry of education in the church. What is hard to decide is what we really think we are about. What's the *place* of church management, the *place* of Christian education in the overall life of the team and its ministry?

5. *Provision is made for authority, responsibility, and accountability.* Notice the rather unusual approach some-one trained to think about systems would bring to this principle. If this system does not have clear lines of authority, responsibility, and accountability, what is the *purpose* of not having them? What benefits does it bring to the system to be vague about who is responsible to whom? Is the system really getting a benefit at the price of its functional effectiveness? Could that benefit be gotten in a less expensive way?

IS EFFECTIVE FUNCTIONING REALLY DESIRED?

We have reached the point where we have to ask a question that may seem silly at first glance. Yet one of the most fundamental principles of systems is that *what happens in a system is what the system intends to have happen.* It is in some ways a harsh principle. In the abstract, it may not seem so harsh, but in concrete situations it means, for example, that when a system is ineffective, that happens because the system *intended* to be ineffective. (That intention may have been carefully kept out of conscious awareness.)

In a few cases that might mean that a congregation or a multiple staff really wants to fail, wants to be ineffective in its functioning. What is more likely, however, is that although a congregation or a team values success and effectiveness, it values something else more highly still.

Consider any one of the principles of effective function-ing just described: having a set of clearly defined goals, for example. A staff might value individual differences so highly that achieving a set of clear goals was seen as disrespectful of individuals. The participants might choose consciously not to try to develop clearly defined goals. At such a point it could be said that the group was placing some other value higher than effective functioning.

Is effective functioning desirable? Perhaps it is not, if it comes at the price of a huge investment of time in achieving consensus about ministry, or at the price of acknowledging that some people in the group have more authority than others. We may wish to have absolute equality in the life of a team, and we may bend our strongest efforts toward achieving such absolute equality. In so doing, perhaps we shall deliberately blur the lines of authority that exist. (It happens quite frequently.) Then, if someone points out that the blurring of lines of authority undercuts effective functioning, it is possible to choose between the two.

That is not a choice I think I would make, but it is a choice with some thoughtful purpose behind it, and some staffs might well choose to make it. What is dangerous is pretending that it is not a necessary choice, that we can have it both ways, that we can completely blur all lines of authority and still have effective functioning.

9

Issues in Multiple Ministry

Early in this book I said that there were a number of issues in multiple ministry today that did not exist when I first studied and wrote about multiple ministry. I want to return to those issues now and discuss them a little more fully. One is the issue of ordained women.

ORDAINED WOMEN IN MULTIPLE MINISTRIES

For decades, unordained women participated in multiple ministries, almost invariably in subservient roles. The subservience did not mean that the *presence* of a woman was unwelcome or that her contributions were seen as unnecessary. Women did a great share of the work in Christian education. They served as advisers to youth groups. In some denominations, women worked at the judicatory level and had immense influence on the life of the church. I can identify more than a dozen Presbyterian ministers, whom I once heard called the Cincinnati Mafia —I'm one of them—who entered the ministry in part because one woman on the staff of Cincinnati Presbytery in the late 1940s saw their potential while they were adolescents and urged them to consider their call.

Were women then not welcome? Were their contributions considered inconsequential? Probably not, yet they could not be ordained, had no structural power. Things changed markedly when women began to be ordained.

What difference did the opening of the ranks of clergy to women make to multiple ministries? It made many differences, of course, although in some ways it still has not made enough difference. First, I invite you to look at one difference often completely disregarded, one that has to do with one of the principal meanings of ordination.

The Making of Ritual

However a particular denomination may use the word "priest," unordained women were not priests in the sense that they were the constructors or architects of *ritual*. Now they are. More than that, their ordination has called upon a previously male society to give up some of its significant rituals and to redesign others. That male culture has not done well with either of those demands; often it has given up old rituals grudgingly but then has not participated with women in the design of new ones.

Earlier in this book I discussed the "three R's": roles, rules, and rituals. For many years, the role of ritual maker was one not available to women on formal or tacit levels. On an informal level, many women did make myth and ritual; but on the level where ritual had psychological power (tacit) or legal force (formal), women were denied this role. The rituals themselves were in the hands of the men. From the construction of eucharistic liturgy to the ritual formalities of a business meeting, men held sway. The death knell of this pattern was sounded with the ordination of women to the ministry of the Word.

An old saying attributed to more than one poet says, "I don't care who writes a nation's laws as long as I write its songs." Whoever wrote it understood something about the power of ritual. Those who write songs, who create ritual, who have a strong hand in the words and gestures we repeat whenever we gather, have immense influence on our sense of common identity, our understanding of ourselves. So long as women had only a small or an indirect hand in the architecture of ritual, the extent of their influence could be kept under masculine control.

But men and women have not successfully worked together to develop *human*-oriented rituals to take the place of *male*-oriented rituals, and thus a vacuum has developed. (Note that it would be quite inaccurate to blame either the men or the women for this.)

The Presbyterians provide an example showing how a powerful but often unnoticed ritual has disappeared. For decades, it was the custom in (all-male) presbyteries and synods to begin any statement to the governing body with the salutation "Fathers and brethren." The ordination of women brought a completely appropriate end to that tradition. A few voices were heard saying that "fathers" included mothers, and "brethren" included sisters; but they were wrong emotionally and linguistically, and they soon fell silent. But no new salutation has developed to take the place of the old one. A few suggestions have been put forth, and some of them are occasionally used: "Fellow presbyters" is probably the one most often mentioned.[1] A few speakers use it from time to time, but it has no ritual power. "Fathers and brethren" was *ritually* used in the sense I have used the word "ritual" in this book. No one would think of beginning an important statement to a presbytery or synod without invoking that salutation. There is now no phrase Presbyterians use in that way.

The ritual is lost. That seemingly inconsequential salutation bound Presbyterians together and gave them a part of their sense of who they were. Almost nothing in the life of presbyteries and synods offers that bonding power now. In consequence, presbyteries have tended to develop rituals of their own, which, because they are unique to the particular presbytery, function to *separate* presbyteries from each other although perhaps providing significant bonding inside the boundaries.

The vocal techniques men use to make a point differ

from those used by women. Male and female bodies move differently—whether walking down the street or celebrating the Eucharist.

The meaning of this change for multiple staffs is subtle but definite. Certainly the coherence of staffs, and probably their effectiveness, will be enhanced by the development of new rituals at more than one level. At the level of the local congregation and staff, men and women together can create and evolve rituals that symbolize the staff's unity and commitment and provide a bonding force. Before such moves have their full potential impact, however, it will be necessary in the various denominations to develop rituals at judicatory and all-church levels that provide the same sense of bonding. Without the ritual expressions, the bonding will be weak; without the participation of both men and women in the creation of those rituals, it will be a fraud.

Women's Roles Within Staffs

In many cases, the ordination of women has made almost no difference in the nature of their work on a particular church staff. One woman said, "I've been a Director of Christian Education, and I'm *still* a Director of Christian Education, except now I can put on a clerical collar, which I wouldn't wear anyway since it's a man's garment." Other women have pointed out that the only real difference, which is admittedly important, is the ability now to participate in the denomination's pension plan.

To what extent is it the case that the specific kinds of jobs women can get on multiple staffs are little different from the kinds of jobs available to them before ordination became possible? The change is greater than most people think, but smaller than most women clergy hoped for. Certainly some denominations have done considerably better than others in providing opportunities for women to be heads of staff or to preach regularly.

Meanwhile, the *psychological* roles given to women in

multiple ministries are worth noting. To a very large extent, groups dedicated to conflict avoidance have chosen a woman on the staff to be the pourer of oil on troubled waters. Two systems observations immediately come to mind about that: first, that a woman could not be elected to that role unless she accepted it, but, second, that "helping people not to fight" is a role into which many women in American culture have been heavily socialized. Not all women accept election to the role of covering over conflict; some enjoy scrapping, taking part in angry exchanges. An appropriate response to that fact is probably a Prayer of Thanksgiving.

The notorious slowness of systems to change—in fact, their steadfast resistance to change—should remind us that when a change is forced on a system, that system will do its best to keep the change from having much impact. So we should expect that church systems confronted by the ordination of women would work hard—unconsciously, but hard—to keep women doing the same things they have been doing for decades and to keep them out of roles they traditionally have not occupied, such as "preacher" or "head of staff." A friend who is a minister in the new Evangelical Lutheran Church in America ruefully points out that despite the presence of several highly qualified women candidates for the office of bishop on the slates of various districts, every single bishop elected by the new church was a white male between the ages of forty-five and sixty: in other words, the traditional group from which bishops have usually come. (The first replacement for a resigned bishop was, however, a black male.) There is no reason to expect that congregations in the process of selecting staff members in a multiple ministry would act any differently.

The presence of ordained women on multiple staffs may be expected to change the processes and the "feel" of multiple ministries, but the change is most likely to come the way bread dough rises. Sharp, radical changes often seem more desirable; revolution frequently promises more than evolution. But it is evolution that in fact produces genuinely new forms, because it much less often engenders stubborn reactions. A system is always strongest when the roles important to it are available to *all* its members who have the competence to fill those roles.

COUPLES IN MULTIPLE MINISTRIES

Multiple ministry involving couples may take three forms: (1) a co-ministry where both members of the couple have the title "Pastor" and are technically coequal as pastors of a church; (2) a co-ministry where both members of the couple are associate or assistant pastors responsible to another minister who is head of staff; and (3) a ministry where the two are not coequal, but one outranks the other in some way. There are other patterns of life for clergy couples that involve ministering in two separate settings, the way the Denhams did in chapter 7.

Few couples will voluntarily undertake a ministry of the third kind. Almost invariably (there are exceptions) such ministries give the husband the office of pastor and the wife the office of associate or assistant pastor. Congregations using this pattern tend to look very much like the congregations of the days before women's ordination, where a minister's wife acted—and was treated—as an unordained, unpaid assistant pastor.

Patterns in which wife and husband have equal authority and responsibility are more popular with couples. But they are not without serious drawbacks. In fact, the whole business of being a clergy couple has both deep advantages and noteworthy drawbacks, no matter in what location the ministries are undertaken.

The Painful Effect of Togetherness

I once asked a group of clergy couples to participate in the following exercise:

> Imagine that you and your spouse are having dinner together. . . . Get yourselves seated at the table. Now imagine that your spouse keeps looking at you with a rather troubled expression. . . . Now your spouse looks directly at you and says, "I have to tell you something important, something that's been bothering me a lot." Let yourself worry and wonder a little bit about what's coming, before your spouse speaks again: "I have decided that the ministry is not for me. I would be perfectly happy if you continue to be a minister, but I am planning to leave the ministry." Now let yourself feel whatever comes in response to that announcement.

The couples found this a distressing exercise. It focuses on what many couples in ministry together would prefer to avoid: the negative aspects of blending work life and personal life. That blending has both positive and negative aspects, but a significant proportion of couples in ministry together prefer to deny the negative side, pretending that only the positive side exists.

When we form a new family by marriage we enter a process of becoming a dyad, creating a family in which becoming a differentiated self is a challenge. This takes place at a time in life when we have just managed to differentiate ourselves from our families of origin. Being an individual self is, I believe, the single most important aspect of becoming ready for marriage.[2] Suppose now that both members of a couple have the same profession. Although their styles of ministry may differ, they have chosen a shared mutual identity. The option of serving together in a multiple ministry represents considerably more togetherness in ministry than serving in two different locations, but both represent a shared mutual identity. As the guided imagery exercise I undertook with those clergy couples suggested, the abandonment of that identity, when one member of the couple undergoes growth or change, is likely to feel threatening to the other member of the couple. The degree of threat is directly related to the degree to which the couple has experienced a need to form a kind of psychologically homogeneous lump. Ministry for some may represent an acceptable career only if it is also the career choice of the spouse, so that continuing in ministry while married to a partner who is now no longer a minister will make them uneasy.

Conflation

"Conflation" is a term that has cropped up in the studies of celibacy of Catholic priests over the past twenty years. It refers to one of the main problems of rectory life, where priests of the same parish are also living together in the rectory.

In a Catholic parish I once knew, there was a priest I'll call Father Brassard. A well-known problem in the parish was Father Brassard's stew. Beginning on Saturday, Anthony Brassard put all the leftovers from each night's supper into one large pot, and on Thursday evening the entire pot, with whatever was in it, was heated up and served to the parish staff. It is not difficult to imagine why young priests in that parish dreamed about being invited to a parishioner's home for dinner on Thursday. Throughout the week, when priests were working together, the stew would become a matter of discussion. But at meals they often talked about the business of the parish, and the meals turned into staff meetings.

Conflation: dealing with church business at a time when a more appropriate discussion would be personal, or discussing personal affairs while ostensibly doing the business of the church. But it isn't the doing of something at an inappropriate time that's the problem, but rather never being able to separate the two. They get conflated—literally, blown together.

For couples ministering together, the danger of conflation is always present. It is at best difficult for clergy to draw boundaries and to keep a clear distinction between personal life and professional life. The church staff system and the marital system invade each other's boundaries to the detriment of both systems. How can clergy couples maintain a very clear distinction, so that their professional partnership and their personal partnership affect each other as little as possible?

Differentiation

Closely associated with these issues is the need every human individual has for individual development and differentiation. Tightly knit families, enmeshed families, make individuation and differentiation very difficult. So do tightly knit professional groups. If members of multiple staffs think very differently on significant issues, there is always pressure to conform, no matter how dedicated to individual thinking the staff may wish to be. When a couple shares both pulpit and marital bed, individuation does not come easily. The growth of one member of the couple tends simply to replicate the growth of the other. It is hard work to grow in a direction different from that of one's partner; but if we fail to do that, both partners suffer from severe limitations.

Power and Competition

A clergy couple told the story of teaching an adult class together. On one particular evening it was the wife's task to prepare a fairly complicated diagram to clarify some of the points the group would consider. Late in the afternoon, as she was working on the last details of the chart and her husband was preparing supper, she became aware that her menstrual period was starting. Although menstruation did not pose a serious problem for her, it was usually accompanied by moderate discomfort and moderate anxiety. Her husband agreed to present her material at the class, and she was grateful. But as the meeting proceeded, she got in touch with some of her anger, both at her body and at her husband. She decided to make an effort to participate more fully and suddenly realized that a particular point needed making. So she stood up and started to take her teaching role again, making, as it were, a comeback. Her husband promptly declared a coffee break.

The life of any couple is made up of a unique admixture of competition, cooperation, and caring. In cooperation, one assumes there is a significant degree of equality in the relationship. But in both competition and caring, there is a strong sense of a one-up, one-down quality in the relationship. Moments of genuine cooperation and equality are relatively rare, even in the best marriage. Caring can easily masquerade as competition (some people can care for each other only by competing), and competition can masquerade as caring.

That is, of course, also the case with working relationships. One cannot say that power and competition issues are either more important or less important in a work relationship than in a marital relationship; what one can say is that if those two are the same relationship, issues of competition and power are doubly sure to crop up.

When a married couple serves together on the same team or staff, competitive issues in the marriage are unavoidably injected into the system's workings. I have vivid memories of a consultation in a church where the two associate pastors were a clergy couple. The church's pastor, as well as the musicians, educators, and clerical workers, were increasingly irritated with the one-upping that went on constantly. Finally the choir director had had enough. "It's probably not up to me to say this," she said in a grim tone, "but I wish to heaven you two would keep out of this church until you've got your marital problems under control!"

Work Divorces

Work relationships may be entered into with an idealism and romanticism similar to that which marks the beginning of most marriages. If a multiple staff relationship is not working well, ending it may become necessary. But that can happen, and does, when the ministers who need to end their staff relationship with each other are also married to each other, and the marital relationship may be surviving quite well. How might we manage work relationships so that a couple in a multiple ministry can end their work relationship without ending the marriage?

In the cases that have so far been brought to my attention, it has not been possible; the end of the work relationship posed a threat to the marriage that was simply too great. Systems thinking would also suggest that in at least some of these instances a couple with marital difficulties put the stresses into their work relationship until neither the church partnership nor the marital one was big enough to contain the problems.

TOWARD A METAPHOR FOR MULTIPLE MINISTRIES

For more than a quarter of a century I have been observing multiple ministries by several different means: workshops in seminary continuing education settings, denominational meetings and conferences, and consultations with happy and troubled teams and staffs. I have constructed and reconstructed typologies, using terms such as "pyramidal," "laissez-faire," "pure team," and the like. During that period two major metaphors about ministry have occupied center stage for fairly long periods of time.

The first metaphor was the "pastoral director," derived from the work of three creative minds of the 1950s.[3] To many critics of the day, both friendly and unfriendly, that metaphor seemed to point toward a kind of managerial style as the proper style of ministry. Rereading Niebuhr, Williams, and Gustafson's *The Purpose of the Church and Its Ministry* convinces me that the critics misperceived their intent. But the metaphor of the pastoral director, and its managerial implications, hung on for some years until replaced by the metaphor of the "enabler."

The text for those who promoted this metaphor was Ephesians 4:12, which contains the phrase "to equip the saints for the work of ministry." The "real" work of ministry was to be undertaken by the congregation, and the role of an ordained person was to "equip the saints," to make their ministry possible. That metaphor coincided —but it was not merely coincidental—with other phenomena in the life of American churches, including a sharp devaluing of preaching (particularly by seminary students), a negative attitude that often reached sneering proportions toward ministries in parish settings, a withdrawal by most mainline denominations from ministries in college and university settings, and an emphasis on ministry to institutions as over against a ministry to individuals.[4] It appears that that metaphor, as well as the phenomena that went with it, has had its day. But no one is certain what metaphor can replace it.

That concern is very much related to my specific concerns about what makes multiple ministries work well. Work well? Yes, in several senses, some of which I have already discussed. A multiple ministry that works well tends (1) to have some stability over a period of time, (2) to comprise a group of workers who derive satisfaction and even happiness from their work together, and (3) to produce some visible results that lead to the "increase of love of God and neighbor" described by Niebuhr, Williams, and Gustafson.

My observations suggest that a certain pattern in multiple ministry—derived, I think, from a particular metaphor —produces this desirable result. The pattern is the one I have often called the "modified team" approach to multiple ministries. A modified team, unlike a "pure" team, does have a leader. Someone whom we may in our various traditions call the senior pastor or perhaps simply the pastor coordinates the work of the team and takes final responsibility. The others on the team are in some significant way accountable to this person.

But unlike the staff model, the modified team does not

have a blatantly hierarchical structure, with the senior pastor sitting at the top of a pyramid and essentially using the rest of the staff as extensions of himself. (Yes, the congregations using a staff model are exclusively headed by a male, although at the level of higher governing bodies such as presbyteries, districts, or annual conferences there are women who do indeed sit at the top of a strongly hierarchical setup.) In a modified team, there is rich communication among all the members, and the pastor does not act as a controller of those communications. The day-by-day operations, as far as possible, are conducted on a peer basis, and major structures of authority are essentially absent.

And what is the metaphor that can undergird such a model of operations? It is a surprisingly old term, and it has collected some secondary meanings that will have to be cleaned off like barnacles from the hull of a boat that has not been hauled for some time. The original Greek word for the metaphor is *episkopos,* carried over into English, with a psychological barnacle that may need to be scraped off, as "bishop." Its Latin translation (which has also come over more directly into English with some of those unfortunate barnacles) is "supervisor," and the English word with Anglo-Saxon roots (also carrying a barnacle or two) is "overseer." The original Greek and Latin words both imply someone who maintains an over*view* of an entire situation.

We may as well acknowledge the difficulties with this whole set of terms. There are two, and they are closely related.

First is the fact that *any* term or relationship or pattern that gives one person in a system specific authority can always be distorted and used in a way that creates a destructive hierarchy. To "set apart" bishops is not at all the same as to "elevate" them. Bishops, in every system that uses them, can be domineering, authoritarian figures; some are, some are not. But the notion that they are "higher" inevitably invites them to be authoritarian. "Supervisor" is a term little used in church circles, but the same thing can and does happen to supervisors (in churches or elsewhere) as happens to bishops. "Overseer" has to contend with its history as a word used in the slaveholding culture of the early history of the United States.

The second problem, closely related to the first, is that any word with even the slightest hierarchical overtones may be a difficult word for women in the church, who lived for far too long in a broadly hierarchical system in which men were up and women down.

But the answer is not to do away with all situations in which a particular person has leadership or some measure of authority. The only pure teams or co-pastorates I have seen work well (in the terms just suggested) are those in which each member has authority at some particular time, and even those are very few and far between. To do away with all authority in a system throws out the baby with the bath water. And, as George Orwell's *Animal Farm* reminds us, an authoritarian stance invariably comes in the back door when authority has been thrown out the front. I say "invariably" because I have never seen it happen any other way. In the long run, the best solution to the problems of authoritarianism and hierarchy is not to attempt to destroy all authority, but to define it and place it within structures and limits.

In any church large enough to have a multiple ministry there are dozens of ministries of all sorts going on, some of them carried out by ordained staff members, others by unordained staff members, and still others not by staff members at all but by members of the congregation, who may or may not hold a particular office on a committee or board. The pastoral director who would genuinely direct all these ministries can easily become authoritarian, but the enabler who makes them possible (whatever that may mean in a particular setting) is likely to be quite passive.

I am convinced that the model of what I shall here call the overseer (despite the barnacles) is the most useful one for our day. It implies a person who is willing to take responsibility, who tries to maintain an overview of all the ministries being undertaken in a particular congregation, who can make sure that the authority necessary to get a particular job done is in the appropriate hands, lay or clergy, employed or volunteer, officer or member. Such a person sees herself or himself as a member of the system, one who has particular functions (which include leadership and direction at times), but who does not pretend to embody in his or her own person the total ministry of the church.

That is a model with New Testament justification. The men and women closely associated with Jesus were by no means a staff, mere extensions of the one they called Teacher or Master. But they did in fact call him by those titles, which do in fact imply that he had authority. It is an authority we reaffirm when we call Jesus Master or Lord— or Christ.

Notes

Chapter 1: **Multiple Ministries**

1. It may be surprising to read that it is the rebellious Howard Brown rather than Pastor Arthur Jones who is really the authoritarian personality in this instance. Studies of authoritarian personalities, however, make it clear that this is the case. This text is not the place to enter into such a discussion, but two references may be of interest to those who want to investigate further. See T. W. Adorno et al., *The Authoritarian Personality* (New York: W. W. Norton & Co., 1969), and Eric Hoffer, *The True Believer* (New York: Harper & Brothers, 1951).
2. Calling sexism the root of the difficulty reflects a value judgment on my part with which not all readers would agree. One colleague has suggested that it may not be sexism but a form of misguided biblicism; my experience is that most ordained women whom I know would find it difficult to distinguish between the two.
3. Cf. Mary Ann Belenky, *Women's Ways of Knowing* (New York: Harper & Row, 1986), for a creative approach to the differences that may be expected as women and men increasingly work together in church settings.
4. W. R. Bion, *Experiences in Groups* (London: Tavistock Publications, 1951).
5. This approach is well represented by Paul Watzlawick, Janet Helmick Beavin, and Don D. Jackson, *Pragmatics of Human Communication* (New York: W. W. Norton & Co., 1967).
6. Cf. Salvador Minuchin, *Family Kaleidoscope* (Cambridge, Mass.: Harvard University Press, 1984).

7. See Murray Bowen, *Family Therapy in Clinical Practice* (New York: Jason Aronson, 1978).

8. In the motion picture *High Noon,* the sheriff (played by Gary Cooper) protects a community that could have protected itself had its citizens banded together. One man and one woman (his wife, who wants him to reject the demand) are called on to make a sacrifice, while everybody else goes into hiding.

Chapter 2: Learning a New Way of Thinking

1. For many years this concept—the "principle of homeostasis"—was stated flatly, as though there were absolutely no question about it. More recently, however, researchers in such diverse fields as biology, physics, and psychology have suggested an important corrective. The problem is that the principle fails to account for such phenomena as the sudden transformations in some systems, including human interactional systems, analogous to what in physics is sometimes called the "quantum leap." Human interactional systems are in fact capable of sudden major transformations that transcend the principle of staying the same. Those systems—small groups, church staffs, congregations, business organizations, families— *evolve* in response to both external and internal pressures. When a system is pushed far enough off its "balance point" (a point from which it can work to reestablish equilibrium), it then evolves into a form both new and unpredictable. In that light, some family therapists deliberately push families to a point where they can no longer come back to the balance of forces with which they started.

2. Murray Bowen, op. cit. chapter 1, note 7.

3. H. Ross Ashby, *Design for a Brain* (New York: John Wiley & Sons, 1952). Ashby's concepts are thoughtfully applied to human interactional systems by Lynn Hoffman in her book *Foundations of Family Therapy: A Conceptual Framework for System Change* (New York: Basic Books, 1981).

Chapter 3: Roles, Rules, and Rituals

1. Barbara Tuchman, *The March of Folly* (New York: Alfred A. Knopf, 1984).
2. Kenneth R. Mitchell and Herbert E. Anderson, *All Our Losses, All Our Griefs* (Philadelphia: Westminster Press, 1983).
3. Kenneth R. Mitchell, "The Secret Contracts of Marriage," *Menninger Quarterly* 23:13–22 (Fall 1969). Also printed in *Human Sexuality*, R. H. Kirk and B. C. Wallace, eds. (Dubuque: Kendall-Hunt, 1972). Also see Kenneth R. Mitchell, "Tacit Contracts," *Pastoral Psychology* 23:7–18 (March 1972).
4. Although entering into the formal role of mother or father does not involve an "installation ceremony," that is one of the psychological thrusts of the sacrament of baptism as practiced in those Christian bodies using infant baptism. Pastors are well advised to be alert to the fact that parents, particularly when the child is their first, are entering into a new role and a new stage in life, while giving up roles and life-styles they previously had.
5. This quotation is from an unpublished paper by Herbert Anderson, part of a project in preparation by Anderson and the author.
6. The assertion that what actually happens in a system is what the system intended to happen probably needs some brief discussion. It is very close to the well-known dictum that all behavior has meaning. Most accidents (if not all) are not accidents. If my behavior produces a particular effect upon other people, I have to assume this is the effect I wanted to produce, whether I was aware of it or not. Like the saying that democracy is the worst possible form of government with the exception of all the others, this assertion about the meaning of our behavior feels almost unacceptable until we consider the alternatives, all of which are horrifying.
7. The particular areas touched on in the text at this point are suggested by anthropologist Edward T. Hall's classic text for nonanthropologists, *The Silent Language* (New York: Fawcett Premier Books, 1966). Hall thought in systems

terms long before systems thinking was even called by that name. Hall refers to the areas in which systems make rules as Primary Message Systems, a term I avoid here in order to avoid confusion between the same word used with two different meanings. Hall's ten Primary Message Systems are labeled by him as interaction, association, subsistence, bisexuality, territoriality, temporality, learning, play, defense, and exploitation.

8. At Princeton University in the 1950s, it was standard practice to call all entering freshmen to a class meeting in Alexander Hall. There, some of the university's traditions were explained in hortatory fashion. But it was flatly claimed that the university had no particular rules except that students (these were the days before Princeton admitted women) were expected to conduct themselves as *gentlemen* at all times. Despite a certain naïveté, most students immediately and correctly assumed that there were actually many rules for student behavior. As the saying went, "Princeton has no rules, and heaven help you if you break any of them!" This impression was enhanced by the presence of seven proctors (many of whom were retired policemen) who patrolled the campus in the evenings.

9. Hall (op. cit.) calls things so treated *formal* aspects of a culture: we cannot conceive of handling them any other way.

Chapter 4: Studying a Church or a Staff

1. Ludwig von Bertalanffy, *General Systems Theory* (New York: George Braziller, 1968).
2. Edward T. Hall, op. cit. chapter 3, note 7.

Chapter 5: The Self-Study of Pilgrim Church

1. Several actual congregations in the United States are called by this name; this case study does not refer to any of them. The name and the denomination have both been changed.

Chapter 6: **Two Cases in Brief**

1. I have described this church and some of its staff problems previously, in *Psychological and Theological Relationships in Multiple Staff Ministry* (Philadelphia: Westminster Press, 1966). The present description is an example of the way in which new information about the church and its staff, as well as a new approach, gives an expanded understanding of the issues involved.

Chapter 7: **The Anger Bearers: A Consultation**

1. There is, so far as I know, no actual denomination with precisely the political structure described here. Although the case is a real case, certain details have been altered, among them details that would permit identification of "All Saints" or the denomination to which it belongs.
2. The Latin word "visitor" implies someone with the right to come in for a very close look, even without an invitation.
3. The term "workaholic" is often casually used to denote hardworking persons, quite often by those persons themselves. It is not unusual to hear someone describe himself or herself as a workaholic. More often than not, such persons seem to take a kind of pride in the designation. Actually, workaholism is as serious and destructive a disease as alcoholism. The term does not refer to a willingness to work hard, or to a love for one's work, but to an *addiction* that excludes concern for other aspects of living. The workaholic, exactly like the person addicted to alcohol or any other drug, is a sick person. When there is a workaholic occupying a significant place in a system, it is important to understand what function his or her workaholism plays in the system. Thus, to call the pastor in this situation a workaholic is no casual matter.
4. Sculpting, like many other psychologically powerful techniques, can be dangerous if carelessly used. Thoughtfully used, however, it has immense power. It has been used effectively in family therapy for a number of years. Probably the single best reference to the technique is Peggy Papp's "Family Sculpting in Preventive Work with 'Well' Families," *Family Process* 12:197–212 (1973).

5. See Ephesians 4:26–31. Particularly in verse 26 the apostle gives advice that has often been misinterpreted to tell us not to be angry. Actually, the point made in this verse is that we are not to *cherish* our anger.
6. Mitchell and Anderson, op. cit. chapter 3, note 2, p. 80.
7. Although literature exists concerning the theory that behavior taking place within a group is the group's property, it may not be helpful to give citations. The reader is referred to W. R. Bion, op. cit. chapter 1, note 4. Material of this kind is not really learned, however, by reading any source, no matter how good. Participation in the group relations conferences carrying in the United States the name of A. K. Rice or Tavistock, and those in Canada sponsored by the Rose Hill Institute, is the only way the author knows of effectively grasping these ideas.
8. One of my own earliest lessons in family therapy came when I was working with a family while Salvador Minuchin, acting as a consultant, looked on by means of a closed-circuit television system. We used a "bug-in-the-ear" technique by means of which Dr. Minuchin could communicate directly but privately with me. He directed me to "take over" the family, including picking up the family's little three-year-old boy and holding him on my lap. Near the end of the interview Minuchin's voice suddenly sounded in my ear: "Now give the boy back to his father." Later, in a conference, Minuchin pointed out that it was important for me to give authority in the family back to the father, and that this was powerfully symbolized by putting the little boy in his father's arms.

Chapter 8: Principles

1. Kenneth R. Mitchell, *Psychological and Theological Relationships in the Multiple Staff Ministry*, pp. 158–177.
2. Pat Conroy, *The Prince of Tides* (Boston: Houghton Mifflin Co., 1986; Bantam Books, 1987).

Chapter 9: Issues in Multiple Ministry

1. I have heard indirectly that some voices have been raised in protest against the salutation "Fellow presbyters" because

the word "fellow" is a masculine word. From the point of view of those genuinely concerned about language, such a protest is nonsense. Fellow is not a masculine word but comes from an Old Norse word meaning "partner" or "companion." On the other hand, many women use the word "guy," which is a strictly masculine word in origin and ordinary usage, to refer to men, women, and mixed groups. There is deep and powerful irrationality in questions of linguistic gender. Once again, it is necessary to ask what a given word means in a particular system. If in some areas (language systems) the word "fellow" is exclusively associated with males, its use is bound to be offensive to those whose intentions are genuinely inclusive.

2. See Herbert Anderson and Kenneth R. Mitchell, "You Must Leave Before You Can Cleave," *Pastoral Psychology*, vol. 30, no. 2 (Winter 1981), p. 17.

3. H. Richard Niebuhr, Daniel Day Williams, and James M. Gustafson, *The Purpose of the Church and Its Ministry* (New York: Harper & Brothers, 1956).

4. In his essay "Two Royal Children," Dutch pastor Nico ter Linden discusses his experiences as a student chaplain in a prison. "We discovered there in Scheveningen that the whole prison system within which we had to do our work was no good. 'This way we'll never heal anybody,' we cried out, ready to march on Parliament with placards and banners. But our teacher proposed that we should wait a while for that. . . . Later I realized that he had other good reasons to warn us away from tough action for the moment. He must have known that it was an unconscious maneuver on our parts to escape the pain. It feels good to imagine that you're wearing the white hats and the Director of the Department of Corrections is wearing the black one. . . . I think that behind our desire to have a go at the structures of society another impure motive was hidden: flight from hard work to simpler work. To help people 'so that they may be sound in the faith,' to use St. Paul's words, is scut work, as the slang phrase has it. It demands a lot from you, and even more at a time when heaven lies low and the church is in a slump. For a shepherd of souls who's in trouble, political action can be an escape; he can bask in the thought that now he's really doing something for his sheep. It isn't necessarily bad

theology that's behind this new way of operating; he's an up-to-the-minute minister, isn't he, and people outside the church can finally see that not all Christians are in collusion with the existing order." From *Hoeing in the Vineyard,* a translation from the original *Schoffelen in de Wijngaard* (Hilversum: Gooi en Sticht, 1982) now being prepared for American publication.

Index